OVER STONE WATERS

POETRY
by

Jimmy Lowe

Author's Tranquility Press
ATLANTA, GEORGIA

Copyright © 2024 by Jimmy Lowe

All rights reserved. No part of this publication may be reproduced, distributed or transmitted in any form or by any means, including photocopying, recording, or other electronic or mechanical methods, without the prior written permission of the publisher, except in the case of brief quotations embodied in critical reviews and certain other noncommercial uses permitted by copyright law. For permission requests, write to the publisher, addressed "Attention: Permissions Coordinator," at the address below.

Jimmy Lowe/Author's Tranquility Press
3900 N Commerce Dr. Suite 300 #1255
Atlanta, GA 30344, USA
www.authorstranquilitypress.com

Ordering Information:
Quantity sales. Special discounts are available on quantity purchases by corporations, associations, and others. For details, contact the "Special Sales Department" at the address above.

Over Stone Waters / Jimmy Lowe (Corrected and Revised)
Paperback: 978-1-965075-79-1
eBook: 978-1-965075-18-0

SOMETIMES OUR JOURNEYS TAKE US TO
PLACES WHERE THE WATERS ARE ROUGHER
THAN THE STONES; THESE WATER'S SHAPE THOSE WHO
CAN REMAIN IN THE RIVER LONG ENOUGH TO BECOME
POLISHED.

INTRODUCTION

When times presented themselves by a guy getting out of line, being offensive and disrespectful, I would give him the benefit of doubt and avoid the default masculine violence for my environment. Instead, I would quietly and humbly go along my way and write a poem about the event. Then I would return to the guy, if he was able to receive it and read it to him. Most of the time the guy would realize that just maybe he should leave me alone. Otherwise, I have to write to keep balanced, and moreover comprehend life. Much of this work is done to exercise a gift as a hobby. A gift that was given to myself through the wit of my own mother. Three words were put into my head when I was around 3 or 4 years of age: Encyclopedia, Dictionary and Independence. Later, as I learned to read, I found News Papers to be curious and wanted to write as a journalist. It is said that: "You cannot teach a man from your own experience; you can only place him in the position to learn from it; himself". If that is the case, then the whole library and educational system is nil and void. What my writing does is place you in the position to learn from my experiences and the experiences of others. The giver of all good gifts is the living God in the heavens. He will love you and those around you to accomplish his goals. Why should you read this book? That is a good question and I have a good answer. It is recorded in the archives of ancient philosophies that; man, who has experienced many hardships in life finds many valuable lessons. It is these valuable lessons that I hope to share with all who will take the time to listen to what is being read. The impossible... is possible with the living God supporting you. Out of three words came all of this, and much, much more. A few pieces were written in 1982, and 1983: "Married to Misery", "Society" and "Little Brother". As an aspiring writer of nineteen years old, I decided that I would write a song in my head. With that, I decided to write a song like Hank Williams might sing. Moreover, I would make this song about Hank himself, who was a known alcoholic. This is what I got. From two hours of bus came the song "Married to Misery", written in my head without paper to record it on. Thank you for purchasing this book. It is my hope that you continue to enjoy its expression for many years to come, because it is written to encompass your mind. It also illustrates in words that everything does not have to be so complex, and so stressful as we like to make them out to be. Everything in life is a test and every test has a lesson. Each piece in this book has a lesson ... get from it what you may...words are winsome! Please think about what you read... Remember, "Everything in the light has a shadow!"

Contents

INTRODUCTION 1
SOBRIETY 1
I NEED YOUR HAND 2
MY PUPPET 3
SCRIVENER 4
LIFE-FETCHER 5
RUN 6
FREQUENT MODULATOR 7
HOLE IN THE FIRE 9
LOST IN THE BLUES 11
COWBOYS 12
JOUSTING WITH A PEN 13
ONCE UPON THE GROUND 14
RAINY DAY BLOTCHES OF INK 16
WHISKEY WEATHER 17
BIRDS OF RHYTHM 18
FANGS OF INJUSTICE 19
POISONED POOL 21
JUST ONE TRUE APPROBATION 23
HAPPY 25
WORDS ARE WINSOME 26
TROPHY -TROPHY 27
JOKERS PLACE 28
STORM UNDER-GROUND 29
ANOXIC FROST 30

FRET FIELD	31
LEAVES OF LIFE	32
COLD SHAKY HANDS	33
SEDATED	34
YOU	35
HAND IN HAND	36
A LITTLE SPREAD	37
BEYOND BY QUILL	38
DREAM INSIDE	39
SPRY FREE SPIRIT	40
MUSIC TRAIN	41
MEAN AND GREEN	42
THOSE HARD TO FORGET	43
FROM COWS TO COWGIRLS	44
WATERS OVER STONE	45
HEART OF ICE (SOUL OF FIRE)	47
DINGY LAND	49
PICTURE	50
COUSINS (GREED AND DEATH)	51
DEAD DUCKS ON THE HIGHWAY	52
STUNTMAN OF MUSIC	53
"THE MIND"-BIGGER THAN BRONZE	54
COUNSELING MOTHER (PEACEFUL CALM)	55
THE SOLITAIRE	56
MILK BOX FLYER	57
CRAFTED FOR PLEASURE	59
REDWOOD TREES	60

TO THE VISITOR	62
BUBBLES	63
EULOGY OF SUICIDE (SILENT SCREAMS)	64
CHRISTIANS FEEDING CHRISTIANS	65
! APRIL-APRIL MAY-MAY!	66
KEY	67
MINISTERING ANGELS	69
UNITED	70
LEGO LAND (PLASTIC WORLD FOR PLASTIC MAN)	71
FOREVER MORE	73
GOLDEN INK	74
LIFE BY DEATH (MY HEART IS A TITLE WAVE)	75
HAPHAZARD AND HARMONY	76
BURIED DREAMS	77
DEAD MAN'S EYES	78
GUITAR	79
EARLY MORNING MERRY MELODIES	80
LIVING LIFE IN LETTERS	81
HOW	83
THESE FRIGID WALLS	84
BURNING UP MY VOICE	85
LONG GOODBYES-CHEAP TOBACCO	86
MARRIED TO MISERY	87
REGULAR	89
NICE SHORT RIDE	90
TRUE COLORS	91
MITE BREAD AND BUG SOUP	92

CAN NOT SEE THE SUNSET	94
MUSIC IS IN THE EAR OF THE BEHOLDER	95
CRACK MACARONI AND CHEESE	96
WHAT'S OWED	97
MY WORLD	98
A THOUSAND FLAT TIRES	99
COP A SQUAT	101
BORN CRAZY?	102
ROMANCING THE MICROPHONE	103
BEAUTY OF THE STORM	105
RUNAWAY AND THE SILVER TONGUE STRANGER	106
ROCK LEGENDS	107
STRANGER IN YOU	108
MR. DEATH	110
AGE IN YOUTH	111
CANNOT KNOW A PRODUCT (BY THE PITCH OF ITS SALE)	113
SPELLBOUND BY MY MUST	114
UNETHICAL DEED	116
IN THE BLISTER BURNING BLUE	117
REQUIESCAT	118
THE SANDS OF NOUNS	119
A WORKING BOYS CHRISTMAS	120
ON MY JOURNEY BACK	121
DESERTED AGAIN	123
ANTI	125
IF ONLY I, WERE YOU	126
CRAZY EDDIE	127

JUST LET IT GO	128
STAIRWELL TO YOUR CONSCIENCE	129
TITLE TO MY TALE	131
CHANGES IN YOU	132
LITTLE BROTHER	133
PORTABLE SANDBOX	134
BABAMERICA	136
THE FOOL ON THE LOST SEA	137
NOW YOU DID IT	138
TEMPLE OF FAME	140
NEW AGE LIVING	141
XUSK	142
YOU ABORT YOURSELF	144
DEATH BY LOVE	145
THE HYPOCRITE	147
LO, THE POET	148
POSTAL ACCESS TO YOUR HEART	149
LOVE IS…	150
MR. SUNSHINE	151
DOWN WITH KACEY	152
CLEARING FIELDS BY NAILS	154
ALPINE INNER SPIRITS	155
CAUGHT IN A TREND	156
JOKER IN THE DEAL	157
BROKEN ON A STICK	159
FROGGY AND THE ORIOLE	160
LETTER TO A FRIEND	162

THE HUBCAP MAN	165
SALAD OF DREAMS	167
IRON BRICK	169
CONTRAST EMPTINESS	171
SEE NO ALL	173
OPUS	175
MOONBEAM LOVE	176
SNAFU	177
RELIGION	179
NIGHT STOLE MY FACE	180
WE DO NOT SEE	181
UNCLE PAUL	182
SPRYLING	183
FORTY FEET BABY	184
PRISON BULLY	185
THE END	186
SOCIETY	187
NEGATIVITY	188
SIGNATURES	189
MASTER O' FLAWS	190
SACRED DREAM	192
WHEN FUTURE COMES	193
DUCK, DUCK GOOSE	194
ATTIRE ASPIRED	195
STATUE OF WAR	196
NATURES STATEMENT	198
BROWN SCARS	199

UNFAITHFUL FATHER	200
TO REMEMBER	201
REALITY RHYMES	203
HARLOT OF THE ARTS	204
BROKEN GUITAR	205
IN ALL YOUR WAYS	206
I'M ONLY ME	208
CHANGER	209
UNDERWENT TRUST	210
PICK MASTER	211
CHRISTIAN READING	212
MATURE DEW	213
AN INFORMAL SENTIENT	214
RAILS TO GLORIOUS	215
PAST, PRESENT, FUTURE	216
MY FLOWER IS HIS LOVE	217
NO SEEMING	218
CRY PRAISES TO THE LORD	220
WASH MY HEART AT NIGHT	221
BIBLE WISE	222
TEACH ME LEARNING LORD	223
ROBE OF SNOW	224
WONDER NO MORE	225
SIGN OF THE TIMES	226
HE WON'T SUFFER YOU	228
ONE GREAT SONG	229
ONCE UPON A WINDY WAYSIDE	230

DEATH OF A PRIME MINISTER 231
POETS LIFE 232
A CENTURY OF STYLE (EULOGY TO GEORGE BURNS) 234
WHAT HAVE I? 235
THE MAKE PUZZLE THEORY 236
THE CITY DUMP 237
JARGON 238
SEE AMERICA (NEO ART) 239
SLEEP SONG 240
GYPSIES AND THIEVES 241
BREATHING GOWN 242
FLESH 244
AUTHENTICITY 245
PAIN IN HAPPINESS 246
SONNETS AND SIMI SONNETS (APPROXIMATELY 1993-1999) 247

SOBRIETY

I am not your traffic light
I AM the voice in your head
I am not the carburetor
Nor the throttle that you dread

I am no after thought
I am not the shifter you gear
No smoke signal or peace pipe
But I am always here

I am ALWAYS near you;
Looking for a sign;
And admit I often fear you;
Those designs that you mind

I am a history teacher
Of great propriety.
I only watch from the bleachers
All you sporting sprees

I am no rollercoaster
Dropping does not thrill me
I am a steady climb
I AM sobriety.

I NEED YOUR HAND

I hurt my Love, as I'm thinking of you
Painful the relationship this way
So far apart, we are together
Storming the weather, cannot lay
to the meter, flood or feeder;
Dream of our touch so pure one day.

But I do surely stand upright for you
Many gals a clever, want onto my leather
You're the only one proven, so true
Come and get me baby, if I am crazy,
I am crazy for Christ, has gave me you
Oh how much I need you baby, it's true.

I need your hand to hold watching movies
If we don't get too groovy, 'for the movie ends
I need your heart to hold me so dearly
in the world severely so sinking a sand
Standing on the Rock of our salvation
As Jesus Christ our Lord pulls us through each day

I hurt my Love, as I'm thinking of you
Painful the relationship this way
So far apart, we are together
Storming the weather, cannot lay
to the meter, flood or feeder;
Dream of our touch so pure one day.

MY PUPPET

My puppet!
My puppet you were
Made by a puppeteer
Tied to a puppeteer

Your smooth brownish tone
Like polished chestnut
I adored to my sweating brow.
Who are you tied to now?

When gone is the day and dark passes night
Beneath a fermenting sky
Now to walk with another
My Puppet you were.

Together we were one
Without a puppet
The puppeteer is none.
Who are you tied to now?

SCRIVENER

A scrivener spread his carbon dust
Changing a piece of tree to poetry
Turning pure white pages to talk
The anxious meld audience lust
Neither waited, nor did walk
Until revealed the scrivener some form.

Standing to scratch his dramatic brow
Barely tilted his hasty head to show
Paroxysm or pleased
None save the poet, this may know
With laughter large, packed away his mighty pen
In an instant, his words were ceased.

The crowd then oohed and cooed the writer
Patting of back with shaking of hands
Never reason for his laughter
He flung this to the crowd
"If you study the world of stage and sages
You will find what the scrivener sees in pages"

LIFE-FETCHER

In the grass not always greener on the other side
Does the common eye always see before the strike?

Old water rippled around the stranded stones
My family and I were picnicking our clones

Funning and fighting as families all do
Just out getting away from societies chew

My fishing pole ready, anxious for a catch
When along came the demon, a child's life to snatch

Sneaking and creeping across all the ground
Upon my foot as I let go no dog-eared sound

Stepping back as I drew my bamboo sword
With my buck fishing line, I lanced off his gourd

Down by the rivers, water is not alone
The life fetcher seeks to leave stranded and stone.

RUN

I want to run not for pleasure
I want to run not for fun
Am not out running for no lover
I am not running from any gun

There is nothing funny about running baby
There is nothing charming about sweat
Nigh to the finish every muscle goes crazy
Still, you have not accomplished it

I want to run through the mountains
I want to run through the sand
Until the sweat from my body fountains
I am the marathon man

I want to run just for pleasures
Even if it cost me, some pain
I want to run in all weathers
In the heat, in the wind and the rain

There is nothing funny about running baby
Believe it we were all born to sweat
There is no excitement in losing, maybe
You can run 'til you get over it.

FREQUENT MODULATOR

Music time, Here I go
To the only bridge I know
With the only ship that is mine
I search to find
In the stars my comfort zone
I try to help my heart to hone
Like the mime
All alone
On the bridge of my radio.

Here I go, Tracing time
In a light not always lime
I am afloat just let it flow
Winsome wheel
With a future in the blind
What is there that we could find?
Just a radio?
It isn't so
But it is the only place I go

FM trails, Time the clock
This earthling calling Spock
Time to slower, lower sails
Man, the clock
Of this surely though I feel
The wheel will never stop
Tale me so
Man, the clock
Mind the rhythm of the rock

Flying on the frequencies man
Modulate the frown
That seep into my head
Modulate the pounds of time that sit ahead
Modulate the sounds that disturb my "can't stand"
Modulate my memories and all the life I planned
Yeah, I know
It is just a radio
But it's the only life I know
The bridge of the radio
The only place I go!

HOLE IN THE FIRE

When I went down to the river
To do some fishing, for a while
Along came ole man winter
Saying how he hated my style.
Then he tried to run me away
So, I gathered up some burning stones
Poured out a hand full of mighty flame.
Warming a winter ground now
Then settled down to warm up my bones.
There I fell into a terrible sleep
As winter had mighty flame dancing all around.

There is a hole in the fire
Running the hills as happy as a clown
Hole in the fire
He will chase the careless down
So, before you aspire
To set him on the ground
Remember, he has two faces, and one is a liar
He is not all he seems
Hole in the fire
Burning up your dreams

One man settles down for the TV
Checking out some old R. Files
On his doorstep awaited ole sister sleep
She had been knocking for a while
She wants to take him away
Fixed him on a combination
Sipping mud and smoking cigarettes
Sister sleep found his concentration
Then came along cigarettes heat
On his roof dancing like a clown
She burned his whole house down

There's a hole in the fire
He runs the hills happy as clown
Hole in the fire
He will chase the careless down
Before you anxiously aspire
To set him any place around
Beware that he wears two faces one is a liar
Not exactly, what he seems
Hole in the fire
Burning down your dreams.

LOST IN THE BLUES

When God gave out blues, I thought He said shoes
So, I asked Him for an extra pair
I have more now than I will ever use
So much that I go to share

When God gave out pains, I thought He said brains
So, I asked for all He could spare
So much I hurt now, that it drives me insane
Sometimes I feel nothing else there

When God gave out prayer, I thought He said, Bayer
I said, "I'll take enough to deal with this pain'
Just when I think it's all gone, it comes scrambling home
Always to give me a fright

When God gave out pure, I thought He said more
I said, "No more Lord, Please! that's alright."
I'll tell you for sure, I never knew what it was
Now all I have left in my heart is a sore

I'd love to be normal, but it just isn't so
I got pains, no brains, and the blues, I got to go
The moral of the story is simple but true
Be careful what you ask and the things that you do
Keep your ears open, hear what is said to you
Unless you become lost in the blues

I'm lost in the blues, there isn't but one way out
That is to share them with you all my friends
Lost in the blues, the walk never ends Listen to the one telling you
Listen lest you become lost in the blues

COWBOYS

They tell me of many mothers' son
Who fell to their death by the hate of a gun!
Sweating beads of blood with wells of tears
Rock fights, bullet bites, the blood of our peers
Blood of the cowboys. (Refrain)

No lady shared no wealth or fame
The wild, wild west they had to tame
They only did what had to be done
Forty-five Indians with a six gun
Fights of the cowboys. (Refrain)

Herds of cattle up and down the trail
Nights too cold, food too stale
Wind and rain, storms un-frail
Across the Mississippi, horse by the tail
Nature's body fought the cowboys (Refrain)

Riding off, on a whiskey wind
On down around the bend
Into a sober setting sun
He only did what had to be done
Cause he was the cowboy
He was the cowboy (Refrain)

JOUSTING WITH A PEN

Jousting with a pen
Whaling through the knights
Knights of sorrow and loneliness
Crowded by measures to pry

A challenge say by say
Erasing scars on my shield
Armor? Need not any? No!
My one armor? Sureness of point

He is down! There,
One more knight is broken
And all his lancing craftiness
Written off by the health of his pen.

ONCE UPON THE GROUND

I was standing on my heartbeat
The sun had yet to end his round
When a castle in the sky appeared
Made of solid cloud

At the gate, you stood a poor boy
Who was looking for a knight?
But saw there no hand nor king
Though he sure saw the light

"A throne a man", to silence he spent,
"So, to judge this old-world right
My search took me to every land
There is no such gent".

I could not believe my lonely eye
The sun behind me smiling
Above the mount the castle had
A perfect silver lining

Then the wind of the golden west
Heard the poor boys' plea
And whisked away the silver-grey castle
To leave him falling free

Forever place high the poor boy
In the echo, hear his yell
Falling from a castle of cloud
Time will quote justly his tale

Fate haunted stands a webbed-up armor
The good knight is good knight no more
What will be is destiny
Echoes the silent shore

He only dropped his humble chin
Once upon the ground
To watch his castle break and leave
Standing on his heart beat.

RAINY DAY BLOTCHES OF INK

All the sky is blue
So am I without you, I am gray,
You're a rainy day
I was just a pawn in play
I am blue

Now what do I do?
What should I say?
Told my friends we're through, they said, "Your OK"
But that isn't true
I must live this way I grow old.

All winter wind is cold.
So am I so I'm told,
I was turned to stone
Left all alone
I am blue
I wish I'd never known a girl like you

If all the world is a stage
I'm just a torn-out page
Your blotches ink running down my face
All my sky is blue
Now I feel the fool
I've been used.

WHISKEY WEATHER

No windowpane or stereo
In a refrain (winter snow)
My chips are in for another day of Whiskey weather
Erase the night and the cold
Eyes are the stairway to the soul
I'm just a sheet keeping dust from your wedding leather

You're out leading sheep that you make blind
I search for sleep in a battered mind
There is an old Proverb:
"The young bride soon finds her husband broken."
You're leaving me insane today
The same as you did yesterday
"When your ship runs ashore, the sea has spoken."

The microwave has a shot glass form
I care not to say what you adorn
My chips are in, I'm on a binge
Every day is whiskey weather
In a refrain (Rain or sun)
Hair of the dog, chain reaction
What a way to learn, my whole-body burns
I discern that you cover another's leather
And every day for me is whiskey weather

BIRDS OF RHYTHM

Ahem! Ahem! Oriole,
Listen closely to my tale.
Breathing deeply down inside my soul
For which you are my ail,

Rhythm runs a special flow
Your early morning cry,
A bauble that will always grow
When into your own I pry

And muster form your precious tune
An I-so-love-ism high
I'll dedicate it to the moon
Your songs keep me benign.

FANGS OF INJUSTICE

You should be aware of him
He computes the tricks
He's the fangs of injustice
In the jaws of politics

He gave the right to kill a child
After it took a breath
The incision of the doctor's hand
Your right to choose is next

He rips the heart from happiness
And chews the fats of power
Blacks out the poor man's honest eyes
He is a junky, force is his fix.

He beat the drums of election
To the green of society
But for the working blistered hand
He slays opportunity

He broke what plow the farmer used
Burned their houses of toothpicks
He is the face of headless horseman
He put the P in poor and pain

(Refrain verses 1 and 3)

Sipping the wine your dead son shed
For you to sport your golden chain
He will not die 'til God returns.
Clearly, he is insane

He rips the heart from happiness
He's a junky force is his fix
He's the fangs of injustice
In the jaws of politics.

1-17 1995

POISONED POOL

Billy Joe was joyous in his new backyard
With his first best friend Connie Lou.
From rolling in the dirt to first-place mud pies,
In the big hole for the pool

Not in the least like the Beverly Billy's
Some tell-tale made them rich
However, there was something really crude
From some low-down son of a rich

Billy Joe and Connie Lou never had a chance
The danger symbols had long since faded
But the digging in the dirt
Was a child-like romance?

Wasn't supposed to have been found today
Some old toxic sent to the sea
But the greedy made a dollar to lighten his load
"Now another dollar saved is a child's life ruined"
What a bill to owe!

Billy Joe is joyous with his new best friend
They're in peace and harmony
Momma sits crying prayers for their bodies
But the coma is forever sure

Every dollar saved is a child's life ruined
Curiosity kills not only the cat
It's also snatching little lives away
So, a wallet can become fat

Son of a rich so greedy
Now so needy, for a conscious you have no more
You buried your ego in toxic barrels
Below Mother Nature's floor

Billy Joe, I know you, and your friend
Found the fault of a greedy hand
Boy let these words be your mud pie
To mark the conscience of all greedy men
Until the day they die.

JUST ONE TRUE APPROBATION

Yonder stands the poor man
Working fingers to the bone
Always giving in a taking nation
And yet still calls it home.

Just one true approbation
Who can tell where it all came from?
Does it take more strength for working?
Than to sit and learn.

Yonder comes the big man
Stomach always afire
Always gravy' his environment
To what does he aspire?

From where came the approval
That the poor should be over run
Spit fire flying between the times
WHO will defuse the bomb?

Yonder come some in-between's
Mask of glass of rum
I agree with the Iroquois Indians
"All the world belongs to everyone"

Say it is good for morale
Some believe it to be dumb
I know you hear what I'm saying
The Iroquois theory is plumb.

Just one true approbation
So tired of getting chewed upon
Born here in this given nation
Raised on the American tongue.

Container ship consumption
I don't even get the crumbs
Just one true approbation
All the world belongs to everyone

HAPPY

Happy go lucky, just a zip too cool
Making a living off his hustling at pool.
Yonder come his sucker
Pocket in the hand
Rack um up sweet Sally, this one is for you.

Happy go lucky, just a zip too good
Orphaned at thirteen to a stick of wood
A spoken misfortune
Others call it luck
It took a life of practice, should it be understood

Has no concern for what sucker he chose?
Let it be spoken, every night they lose.
Battle of the Big Shot
And Happy underway
Rack um up sweet Sally, it's a beautiful day.

Bar tender say, "Happy, I know you're the best
The day winged in; it is time to pass the test
I will back you all the way
Just keep placing that shot.
You will, I know, because you are the best."

"Rack um up sweet Sally, this one is for you
We're running off to Paris, when this test is through.
Rack um sweet Sally
I make history today
Look out Paris, happy Sally is on her way.

04-26-1995

WORDS ARE WINSOME

To basic kinds of writing
Delightful minds go winging.
Like Narration or Description
Spins yarns, or describe real or fiction
With detail of some we loan. Next is Exposition,
Requiring meat for its bones
Some sound old explanations
(The reasons for the happenings
Distinguishes a part of
Object, or classifies clones
Compares an object to the next.
Works may be one or the other
Description or Narration)
Up next, a kind of brother,
Are cousins in a set:
Argument and Persuasion,
Establishing the … mint of
The truth or statement.
Persuasion wants us, these
Comments Accept or
Take actions they support.
The Essays features tell us
Some certain idea (Thesis)
Transitions, like transmissions
In paragraph of giraffes
And sentences within wide
And all organized.

01-21-1995

TROPHY -TROPHY

Trophy, trophy on the mantel wall
Who is the fastest runner of us all?
Trophy leaped from sitting
Then sped down the hall

"Oh runner, runner I mustn't lie
The angels of heaven, up in the sky
You can't outrun, you understand
But you will never be left by mortal man.

JOKERS PLACE

"For all that is done Have I allowed"?
Said the joker to the Ace
"Throw me aside, for what games you play
Do you think you can hide my face?

Stand by your Jack and King
All around, around your Queen
While the numbers flush your face
And when the dancing all is done
You will come back to the one
Standing alone in his place

You figure it as a big thing
And feel that I'm in the dark
Are not your games so new or strange?
I've played them everyone!
Both for greed and fun
Now the joker-jest your mark.

Do not play with me
You cannot sit me free
This box is my only state
Throw me aside while you ware away.
The joker's jester is clear, I will be here
When you meet your worn, final fate
When you make that final play.

STORM UNDER-GROUND

Running for the exit
A storm under ground
She did not give a warning
Just started shaking down

People everywhere were fearing
Running for their life
Mother lost a brother
Husband lost a wife

There seconds dropped a city
Just started shaking down
She doesn't have no pity
The storm under ground

All powers were defeated
Death all over town
Angelinos' been degraded
Storm under ground

"Shall be quakes in diver's places,"
The only book that's' sound
It's there in our faces
Storm underground.

ANOXIC FROST

Water, touch my tongue
Take away this anoxic taste
Quietly in haste
I've been tasting fire since before I was one

Perception of the numbers
Have not the weight to mass
Over this anoxic frost
To keep tasting fire could become a task

Anoxic frost is from toxic water
Like gangrene on my grass
Drying up my taste buds
It even killed my ass

Water, touch my tongue
Anoxic frost just isn't wet
Dry as fire it has become
I hope you're not anoxic yet

Anoxic frost from toxic water
Like gangrene on my grass
Drying up my taste buds
Anoxic water isn't wet

FRET FIELD

All in all, but yesterday
Found me a field where I can say
Fretting nothing, strung up high
Chords of tension where I lose my mind

Summer heat, wind and rain
Old swamp smelling like rotten grain
I notice something, I'm musically high
Where I lay my head, I lose my mind

Fingertips and the silver strings
Together portray all my pangs
Fretting nothing, strung up high
Where I lay my head, I lose my mind.

LEAVES OF LIFE

Are our bodies much like the trees?
Roots touring the depths of our minds,
Absorbing what needs that make it grow.
Our spines-the trunk, are strong and weak,
Supporting what may flourish from the heart.
Carrying daily the leaves of life.
Unlike the tree with no breath.
Spring is the time when seeds are planted.
Summer is the season when we mature,
Growing into weeds or flowers, pretty or ugly.
Autumn has these plants to take on many colors,
Of goods and bad, before falling away for lack of food.
Then there is winter, the coldest most scary of seasons.
This season we are laid out before the cold lonely clay
Taking to heaven or hell that which fall leaves our soul.
Much like the trees, our flesh is used;
Some dead and still blowing in the wind
Leaves of life blossom everywhere.

COLD SHAKY HANDS

His pain is laughter, say weary eyes
He once was happy, now lonely and shy.
Then he could laugh loud, stand straight, and tall
Happiness only comes now when he has to crawl

His friend is his enemy, say cold shaky hands
Without his foes comfort, he just couldn't stand
Standing tall only when, unable to walk
Conversation is useless, he doesn't care for talk

His pain is laughter, your smile makes him sore
When he has to hear laughter, he drinks even more
Drinking to help all his feeling subside
Consequently, he's living on, dying inside

His pain is laughter, say dead empty eyes
What more to be after, a heart sore and sad
The wino called Pappy, has cold shaky hands
Driven stone crazy by the women he had

SEDATED

The air is turning chilly
My feet are feeling cold
It may sound a little silly
But this is getting old
A light burns up ahead
I see a ladder of gold
Tried to move my helpless hand
But I can't seem to get a hold

The silence? Very special!
Like none I heard before
Feels kind of lethal
Is beginning to bore
Into my consciousness
My spirit tries to soar
I can see my way to egress
I can't move to touch the floor

Uneasy voices make me nervous
Guess I seem a little mad
Doc yelled, "He is delirious!"
Cause I fought the drugs he had
Shaking my feet to reassure
That I wasn't dead
Trying to prove, my mind is not sore
But I can't get up out of bed.

YOU

Peaches and pears
All your little cares
Your kiss is sweeter than fruit

Lions and bears
All of your awares
Our love is stronger than the truth

Pork chops and beef
All I love to eat
Your love is more nourishing than health

Diamonds and gold
A fashion too old
I adore you more than wealth.

Plastic and straw
With all I strain
I'm weaker to true love than wet paper chains

Cabins and brick
A heart sore sick
Without your love darling, I'm going insane.

HAND IN HAND

Hand in hand they share all together
Dancing along the corridors of life.
A world-renowned usual couple
Whose marriage license are written on marble.
They lived on my street before
The life of the party; talk of the town.
I have saw them at sunset waltzing around
Dancing on the beach front
Full of false pleasures and laughs.
At the Monday breakfast table In tinkling glass.
Hand in hand they share all together
Dancing in the corridors of your life
I watch them meat manias at the market
They have no better half
They will never divorce, a marriage that is final.
You can take them any place for a ducat
And they will beat you each time
Take your loved ones, run your friends away
Replacing them with ashes and dark glass
They cut the spirit and soul in half
AS you dance with the devil
Down the corridors of life
Alcohol and marijuana are husband and wife.

A LITTLE SPREAD

Planters on the stairwell send messages to passers by
Like, "Here is a happy couple", hid behind these blinds.
But they don't hear the Honky-Tonk or drink the tears I cry
They're not the ones who awake when the children cry.

A hot dog isn't a hot dog without some mustard spread
A burger isn't a burger without mayo on the bread
A marriage isn't a marriage without some hope ahead
No, a marriage isn't a marriage without love.

Voices in the air when we're down at the mall
And well you make believe, when we're visited by friends
I know it wasn't mother, since the bill records each call
But every delicious sandwich must come to an end.

Pictures of the body have not magic enough to mend
The echoes of my heart forever repeat alibis
Ain't no spread could make me swallow, any more of your lies
To the dogs with your rotten heart, I will swallow no more pride

A hot dog isn't a hot dog without some mustard spread
Hamburgers are not burgers without mayo on the bread
A marriage isn't a marriage without some hope ahead
No, a marriage isn't a marriage without a little spread.

BEYOND BY QUILL

I've got a hanker I got to feel
It's time to reach
Beyond by quill

Hear the waters'
Bodies calling
Pages reach
Full blooming

Crowded paper
Stay no more
Walk my conscious
Corridors

Call the cater
Bring my wine
It's time to leave
Those chains behind

DREAM INSIDE

Lad gives his life
To something inside.
To have to live your life
With a boiling dream inside
Who will never grant you rest!
What volcanic showers in the chest!
But live your life with a page in your hand.
Bleeding through your fingertips to understand.
Bringing down to your hand all angers and luv.
Pushing life from a pen to substitute for love.
Pulling toward without from within, that searing knife.
To invite muse to loan his heart to your life.
Your always in a thought, in a struggle.
Your emotions are a path of jungle.
Shelving each dark critical scene.
Shape up an elusive dream.
There too wet down your strife.
To live your small life.
In a big dream!

SPRY FREE SPIRIT

I remember when they'd bring ole Slue Foot
How he panted there all covered in sweat
And I recall how I thought it was so cruel
"But it's no worse than when we fought the Indians",
So, I was told. Now I'm telling you!

Before we brushed ole Slue Foot, I got to ride him
To walk out his run after he'd won
And I could have sworn as I stood there beside him
That he knew the future, the secret of a fall
Would make him an early gun

One dry, warm, windy day in the late of Springs May
(It must have been before they ran him down)
So spry and free, like a fresh summers breeze
He was a happy horse, so ready that day to run
It was then that he knew, that I'd save ole Slue Foot from the pound

Nobody figured it was me; that I set a top rank racehorse free
So, I'll let it be known, Yes! I too learned from the Indians
To watch your back, always cover your tracks'
How such a fiery spirit should always be free

Now it all depends on how you see,
The highlight of my life
Was the day all my family downgraded me
And Slue Foot gave thanks, by giving me a wife
But that is a whole separate story.

MUSIC TRAIN

Every song keeps getting better, whether under the weather
Or riding the leather of a local motive
Crossing the planes, racing the Indians
For a destiny of death to win

Since time began, songs keep getting better
Like a rolling locomotive pushing onward
Climbing to empty my freight
With a load of music on my soul

Rocking and writing to some distant fate
Phenomenal writing rhythms do not wait
Cause the train must always be on time
Rock and write that music into place

Every song keeps getting better, down to the meter.
It is a half a cargo to carry the letter
One the world will taste and never tote
But the scrivener is the antidote

There, sing aloud now, it doesn't sound meanish
It is OK to pour your tongue out; I will only get better
Pour out your soul to my paper and pen
The music train has been rolling since time began.

MEAN AND GREEN

We grew up learning hate and love,
Wondering who lived on the hill above.
Daddy never let us find out,
Exactly what life is all about?

We grew up and we grew up mean,
Grew up loud, grew up mean.
Riot with the forest late at night
Indians and cowboys, reliving the fight.

We learned all the hard way, when daddy died
The joint is a big teacher for a kid with big pride.
Daddy never let us find out
Exactly what life was all about?

Frank and Jessie were two spry youth.
Wabash Cannon Ball, telephone booths.
We grew up loud and we grew up mean.
We grew up loud and we grew up green.

Big brother's world... the penitentiary.
For half his life, he's never been free.
Cause daddy never told us about price.
For loving, another man's wife.

The old man never taught us what it's all about.
There are just some things you must figure out.
We grew up wild and we grew up mean,
We grew up loud and we grew up man.

THOSE HARD TO FORGET

Standing out in your mind like trees on the water
Like Omni-noises of a world storm deep into the ear
So too, do those of memory flood our thoughts?
Some with emotions of experience from times ago
Others with only an image
Each emotion with a new experience in our world

Abreast the heart and blanket the mind
Those hard to forget sometimes decease, yet never die
Although others already dead, are yet to pass on
Unseen, except in dreams
Never to leave, leaving different impressions
With a barrier called yesterday, they are out of reach

Some are a beauty of flowers among the colors of life
Others? Mud beneath the puddle on the sidewalk of doom
Where many stops to cool their heels before traveling on,
To meet the others
Those hard to forget never leave us alone
Lifetime's come and go to leave us
Those hard to forget, who leave us alone.

FROM COWS TO COWGIRLS

Who wondered the range was Johnny the wrangler?
A searching for him a fair maid.
Driving home cattle and breaking them broncos.
By shots of whiskey sometimes he was paid.

Young Lisa was lonely and needed a lover
Her poor heart was brandished by fear of the age-
That toggled and pulled; pulled down her dear mother
Young Lisa dreamed of some cowboy to come and take her away.

Her Papa was workman of a lonesome Texas farm,
Who ran off every stranger as he tried to give Lisa away!
"She's been money hungry since she was ten. I've been broken ever since.
Somebody please take her? She's ripped of romance. Somebody please take her away?"

One Texas sunset came along Johnny,
Merry like coyotes, howling for the moon
In the singsong of the saddle, life drifting along;
He took Lisa from dreaming' and gave her a home.

No longer a dreamer: John works his own farm.
But cries the song of his wives' father:
They have been money hungry since ten.
Lawd I've been broken ever since.
Somebody take them? they're ready for dance.
Somebody please, some wrangler come.
Somebody please take them away?

WATERS OVER STONE

When I heard her say?
"I must go away
Living is hard my son
Everybody has their day
Your time has come to be a man"
So, I turned to Endorphins to help me understand

Words are water over stones That is all she had to give.
My silver spoon, it was the moon Up above my head
The moon already shared so much
That walking through the darkness is where I learned to live.

"And never spend your breath Solely after wealth
Life is not a pun
You can only be as good as your health.
I will be back for my boys
Stiffen your upper lip, it is time to put away your toys"

Those waters over stone
Splashed about my mind
"Become somebody, sons"
At my request, I went left alone
"Remember now, to animals be kind
"You cannot feed us without father, Mother, leave us behind"

Waters over stone Is all she owned?
All she gave her sons
What she gave is more than words, is true
So, all she gave I learned to use
At my request I was at home alone

Waters over stone May they now ease Mothers Heart?
You gave me more than you realized
Lady, you gave me art
Waters over stone keeps the marble from my heart.
Over Stone Waters.

HEART OF ICE
(SOUL OF FIRE)

Now Linda loved her boys.
All her neighbors express.
"Of her many joys
(They would say)
Her sons were her best.

She gave them everything...
Of want and need, they would not.
To keep them through dread divorce.
Lawd! How she fought.

But the women sure need plenty,
To satisfy her soul,
She found the one
To key her lock.
Pick her form depressions foul.

Her Linda was in love again.
That once to never be.
And age was coming fast-
Err by the way.
She was twenty... soon, show twenty-three.

The new prince of her life,
Agreed that she
May been his wife,
Save her little boys:
Whom he could not see.

Time hoarsely flowed the course of time.
A rewind in Linda's head.
"I could have love once more...
Was it not for?
Would I have to give up my kids?"

A tragedy befell Linda!
In mental brood of day
Two-face! In one mask!
With only one a' showing,
Took her boys away!!!

A search abroad the states
Revealed no "cruel-two."
But one wicked lady
Awaits the fate
Of such inhuman an act to do.

Now two innocent lives,
Cried forth from the Lake.
"MOTHER WHY......
Our live you take?"
Until she could not stand no more...
Linda loved her boys' Police confess.
She could not take the pressure
Of her own measure
She broke down and confessed!

DINGY LAND

Another day in dingy land.
No rides, no fairs, no ticket stands:
No Ferris wheel, just a merry-go-round
And plenty of outstretched hands.

A circus not for show
No audience to please
Animals that walk upright
And punks that think they tease.

The games aren't all illusion,
They are meant to take away:
Create havoc and confusion.
Still here at the end of day.

Brown that stresses reform-
Too determined not to change.
Eight hours forlorn
Three times a day.

Cats who think they are slicker
Then the swamps around this place.
I've have heard tell yah
One can smell yah
Fifty feet away.

Another day in dingy land
A circus not for show
The games are not all illusion
The clock forever goes.

PICTURE

I cut your photo from a magazine
Plastered your face upon my wall
You will never know me or see me
Or know that I took a fall

But you are the closest thing to a woman
That I have had these last long years
You have pulled me through some tough times
And strengthened all my fears

You do not hear my pooling
When I whine and cry at night
Lady I am not fooling, you really keep me sane
If I only knew your name!

I have told you all my deepest secrets
My entire life, with you I shared
You're in my dreams, when I sleep at night
But all you do is stare!

I cut your photo from my magazine
You're faded now, corners frayed
But for as long as you are there
I seem to have it made

If you ever feel as if you're being watched
(We all do just as well)
Lady just don't shun it
For it is only I... here in my somber cell.

COUSINS
(GREED AND DEATH)

Said the wallet to the rose
"Do consider these and those!
All these things that lie between us.
Everywhere the world has seen us.

Do you really think they know?
Are they gonna buy the show?
All who live with me are really losers.
Still, they cannot see, we are partners!

The rose then spoke-on his behalf
(A happy coyish laugh)
"You play the part so well. You champ!
As he did dance, a little stamp.

Just stick with me to be a star
They do not know who you really are.
See! A master plan I have in store.
Go! Start another war!"

DEAD DUCKS ON THE HIGHWAY

Screeching wheels slid; the monster ran them down
Twelve there were: two tumbled, bounced around.
Ten all hugged tightly, fearing death in the air.
Brave as warlords die, mother chanced her fate.

She dropped to her chest from running, dashed and slid.
Knocking limp babies to the clear.
Shouted all..."Flee death", Mom had left their side =
I saw her in her panic; life was her care.

Mother do not leave us, must have been their cry.
There was no father, when from home to keep.
Just a deep running passion, was her drive.
No human alive have I seen to display such care.

STUNTMAN OF MUSIC

While he strains in sweat of light
Acting out the feelings of songs I write
A ghost unseen I live the pain
That make songs for hearts, all around the dial.

Call me the stuntman of music
Taken the hardest falls
An unseen runner in the race
I am the stuntman of music
No number, no name, no face.

Another new heartbreak is on the jukebox
You must have that one for your own
Bragging on the big band, without thought of the hand:
Mr. Metaphor, the stuntman of the song.

Call me the stuntman of music
Taken the hardest falls
The unseen runner in the race
I am the stuntman of music
No number, no name, no face.

So, when you hear a coyote western cry
Solute the men who coin the rhymes
Washing out a solid country song
I am the jukebox bar room hero
You're all welcome world, to tag along.

Call me the stuntman of music
I got no fans who call
The unnoticed runner in the race
The stuntman of music
It is just some music law
NO number, NO name, NO face

"THE MIND"-BIGGER THAN BRONZE

Build thou vocabulary sir
Search thine drab librar y 'fir'
There are vast amounts of knowledge there
Those words that count as knowledge Dare
To give her time - Yes carry her.

Imbed her taste in all you do
Till reddened eyes fall asleep through
Thy studies by hours of work done.
She's given there, go get you some.
Loves-in-wars fare! So 'tis for you.

Vocabulary! Grow your mind.
The bodies weak compared to thine.
Sure, naught but free to hustle 'round
For what hath thee when muscles bound?
On the contrary, two combined...

Written /
© August 30, 1992

COUNSELING MOTHER
(PEACEFUL CALM)

The tress so green, a sky that blue.
Cloud gaiety gray, just grazing through.
Flowers tilted spring to life,
When the sun begins its climbing height.

Bird whistles preach in unknown tongue.
Testify to all Gods powers done.
River's wonder 'long their way,
Ponder where to rest someday...

Remind us that all man's strength
Is as stable only as, life's length
So, when at rest, allay we through
By Gods, own strength alone we will make it to-

Heaven is where Beauties' forever
The pains of life to God more-never.
Therefore, we keep our hearts in Gods great palm
To receive our part of, the peaceful calm.

© 9-18-1992

THE SOLITAIRE

No solitude for the solitaire
Another step along a stair
That has difference non-a' more
'Nether shell on oceans floor
Thoughts-n-eyes, all coincide
And occupy illusions pry.
Stress will vest emotions home.
All alone the solitaire.
No solitude his space must share.

Words a' lure entice despair
And stricken deep to un-compare
Scratch but surface of burdens bared.
Oh, tone, tone, Atone!
With the help of God Almighty thee
I will but spawn this faint degree
By the storms that very
That tries the sea.

Ah solitude within but whence
I strain to espy but a glimpse
Far be it not from I
To find you in some page's writ
These solitaire times
A fist of fingers tender print
Is solitude for the solitaire.

MILK BOX FLYER

My dad he thinks I'm crazy
Momma fights and calls him liar
Now I see my careless face
On a milk jug flyer.

But I'm hanging with the Fifth Street
Everything is cool
Friends Momma wouldn't like to meet.
I've been acting like a fool.

Living up to my father
His very Omni-words
Drinking crack of cocaine
And smoking Thunderbird.

Everything is jazzy
If I want a lay, I'll buy her
Oh, but then, she broke my grin
When I heard her say?
"Call your momma boy; on the milk box flyer".

I want to drop a quarter...
But I'm having so much fun
And it would be a shame
To put my friends under the gun.

It could never happen to me
So, I just kept getting higher.
Now mommas last photo of her son
Is the one, on a MILK BOX FLYER.

Every day I am beside her
But she no longer hears my words
She'll not hold her son again
Thanks to Thunderbird

Poppa says that she'd gone crazy
I know now for sure that he is a liar
Oh, how she must have loved her son
To frame a MILK BOX FLYER!!!

I was hanging with the fella's
And hanging kind of loose
When along came the neighbor gang
Trigger finger in the noose

A flyer like me pulled the trigger
So, he could walk a little bigger
And make lots of money
Selling gypsy juice

Now he sits in prison
I just forever wait
I knew that Christ has risen
Now I face my fate
The only chance is when you're living
I would not suggest that you wait

Let me give you this before I leave you
"I hope to be a satisfier.
You need to call your family
If you're on a milk box flyer

Tough is just a bluff
Everyone is a crier
If the next place, you see your face
Is on a milk box flyer
Call home! Some body cries for you."

CRAFTED FOR PLEASURE

Crafted for pleasure
Molded for love
Mammas little treasure
A jewel form above

Came into the world
By the hands of an angel
Hair of silk gold
All has gone well

Mammas little angel
Crafted for love
Crafted for pleasure
When given her shove

Mammas little angel
Once so proud of
Now with a stranger
Molded to love

Out by the bright lights
Corners and Buzz
No stranger to hot nights
For getting what was

Mammas little angel
Now ready for hire
The coldest of hearts now
Ignite her fire

Many are the dangers
Before you shove
Mammas lil' angels
Are crafted for love.

REDWOOD TREES

Think the trees should deserve
Abuses man enslaves?
Many thousands of years, earth
Has kept them, from the grave.
So remarkably rare.
Not just anywhere found.
To reach high into the air,
From deep below the mound.

The old evergreens hue
To protest," Who has cared?"
While men try and construe
Their amount of age bared
Sawing and chopping they cut them down.
Most torn to mere splinter
For some heat they have burned through
Longest nights of winter.

"Save the Redwood!"
Bulletin boards exclaim.
Mother Nature's truly 'against
Man's cold heart, gone untamed.
Meanwhile forest, "Hold Fast
To your ancient pride; The Giant".
To all except the saw, they
Have stood defiant.

"Save the redwood!" I too
Hue and cry. Since earths birth.
Though earths quakes and storms intrude
The big tree in its hearth
Has survived. Save the Redwood.
Do not yawl destroy
Let them stand and be proud
Such, in its marvelous mirth
Meant for beauty; not for worth.

TO THE VISITOR

Come by the way yon family fair
View the hearts of grim despair
Come to hold the hollow hand
Talk in depth to a shallow man

Hear the voices murmured grievance
See the burdens bare, chest a-heave since
Don't leave me! Though all must
Those outside loves are all to trust.

Come view the sight of man done strayed
See wearied nights, not one has prayed
Trace the cheeks finger, catch the tear
A man in prison by one so dear.

Come by the way kin, family
Come not to stay as been with me
Bring news of the latest in my hometown
To cheer the sluggard, buried on ground.

BUBBLES

Airdrops atop the waters dance
So, pillow soft and precious chance
To exist some seconds, few but more
Sure, to be found on oceans floor

That clear world, think not to smash
Sometimes doubled in a splash
Where children laugh and play or sing
Airdrops are doubled, summer, spring

A pool, the bath, a brook or stream
A happy eye there, joyous gleam
Jumped up to shine by blurp of rain
On windows dried even to stain

Yes! Dance across the waters free
But for a heartbeat, tough then spree
The Count, a child or the Queen
Where there's an eye, bubbles may be seen.

EULOGY OF SUICIDE
(SILENT SCREAMS)

Woe! Who can help him now?
Cold clay does hold his hand!
What grief did bead that brow?
Who will ever understand?

Might rather he had been found???
Yet none would happen by
Till limp, above the ground
He hung there 'till he died

Steel walls did scarcely notice
That dead-end to all his dreams
Lying still, as the ground
Deafens all, his silent dreams.

CHRISTIANS FEEDING CHRISTIANS

Watching the little birds
(I will try and say in fewest words)
Feeding, feeding, feeding their young
Constantly feeding their young

On an egg she sat until hatched
Mom waits 'till fear is smashed
Her patience justly rewarded.
Our lack of it as just distorted

The young! What should we feed?
Mother bird sings that secret need
"Look and learn", I hear resound
Searching, searching, searching indeed.

! APRIL-APRIL MAY-MAY!

April, April, your lights fill my sky
April, April, your lights fill my sky
Let me get a light from your flower
I will brighten up your eyes

Hey May, Hey May can I be your first bloom
Hey May, Hey May can I be your first bloom
Let me snip you from your root stem
I will give you all my room

April, April, wet me with your rain
April, April, wet me with your rain
Shower me with your heart girl
I will be your walking cane

Hey May, Hey May, let me sniff your rose
Hey May, Hey May, let me sniff your rose
If you decorate my garden
I will keep all your algae, newly froze

April, April, let me sip your wine
April, April, let me sip your wine
Let your flower cure what ails me
Then we will be a garden; for all, of time...

KEY

It came about so long ago
Dished out gifts turned from yeah to no
Talents tasted and how they moved
Talents wasted for how they soothed

No love invested, only fun
By hate arrested, all else shunned
The beat of chores changed to sin
Traded a soul for worldly win

From verse to chores to video
From worse to evil shows
They call it music, mutilated minds
Yet it is worship by the blind

Many bare the curse across the dial
Since time began 'till the final trial
In harps, horns, pipes or pounds
Relaxed chants of soothing sounds

Laxed and laid back in the muse
Their minds attached by visions confuse
And bid the watching public, a zoo
Beneath yon jesters dancing shoe

Colliding the after mass
Spin their web for un-damped baths
Shouting for joy of how their spun
Relinquished good heat of the sun

So, pounding heart alert insides
Talents alone bring naught but pride
Take not up, Gods gifts one by one
Lest inherits hell instead of Son

Look abreast at scores, far and wide
Bang their heads until they died
Heard no parent had no laws
"Youth went wild", the famous caw

Headed when they heard its cry
Head over heels and prone to die
Careful now, collect this thought
Time tells all, Eternity has fought

Every life issued has a deed
Trade or sale, or give away naught
Don't sale your soul, for you will see
It is your pass to enter heaven
Without the soul, music is,
The Wrong key.

MINISTERING ANGELS

The angels of heaven have ministered
Unto me:
Gods Free Spirit Testified of
His Majesty.
For in my sleep,
A song I heard,
Magnifying Gods, Cleansing Word.
As I Awoke,
In stark amaze-
Meant the Lord for me,
To understand His ways,
Brief and sweet He did explain:
Shallow or deep,
HE will sustain.

© Feb. 1993

UNITED

United will never mean riots
OR feuds with a neighbor that's
Just not the same
It would never mean that some go hungry
On the street, when there's plenty
To go around:
Does not mean conflicts over prayer
But peace, and love...everywhere
Old Glory Flies.

LEGO LAND
(PLASTIC WORLD FOR PLASTIC MAN)

There wasn't much of daylight left
When the old man crossed the street
Call it perception or call it chance
He thought of those we chance to meet
His back was tired, from working hard
And the final cap in his romance
Led him to trace his feet

The runaway
Just wondered lonely
Dreaming for summer's heat
Call it perception or by chance
He thought of those we chance to meet
As an arrow bent, to the ground he went
But from the fear of father's lance
In the guise of Lego land, the two chances to meet

There weren't any curtains up
In their windows you could see
Both were toting empty cups, faking reality
There was no overflowing, save concepts of knowing
They were rowing on the river named...
"OUTCAST OF SOCIETY"

The tired wrinkled face tilted sideways
A neither chanced a move
"My place is over yonder
If by chance, you wonder
Where an old man like myself might live
I perceive your hungry son, but I have no money
But burrow below the cold cardboard
It's as warm as any stove

In Lego land, as it's been called
Cardboard sets the stage
Realities deception is
A plastic world for a plastic man, In a plastic age.
But I'm for certain, you're a hurting'
Families are often too caustic.
But I'm not one to be a sage.

There wasn't much of morning left
When the old man crossed the street
Through youthful eyes, he beheld the skies
Then felt a shuffle in his feet.
By an angle trip, on the curb he slept
Always at rest, in them youthful scarlet eyes.

In Lego land, as it's been called
Cardboard sets the stage.
One never knows when one may fall
Or who pays the scarlet wage.
But remember when you're knowing
That you are rowing on river
"Outcast of Society"
Even plastic winos can be a sage.

© Nov. 1995

FOREVER MORE

It was the end of June
Beneath a midnight moon
All the stars were shining bright
I held her in my arms 'And told her many charms
She was mine for all my life

The waters rhythm clapped along
Which became our song!
As we danced together in moonlight
With sand in our toes
And our summer clothes
Holding hands just felt so right

 It was love for sure
Began on the shore
It hasn't gone away yet.
She is in my heart
Who had no choice but part!
So, will she be forever-more

No longer can I go to the beach
As the ocean never sleeps
Each try reminds me I am alone.
It was there I found true love
It was there she departed
There is where, I became grown.

GOLDEN INK

There is a never-ending surging
From deep within my soul
Sounding out what stories I hear told.
There is an ever-running stream
Where audit liquids are of gold
When I set my pen to paper Lord,
That golden ink just flows.

There is a never-ending story
Down deep inside my heart
Bending toward the powers to make art
There is an ever-running dream
Where a punning clause may start
When I set my pen to parchment
Smoldering lights I hold

I have a never dying love for a beautiful girl
Pushing me to the thin line called the edge
Cause she is no longer any part
Of my thinning linear world
I can only live without her
To have her living inside of me
In my music as the bridge

I got golden ink within my pen.
To so many it seems bleak,
Or blue or red.
But this ink is made of gold
Because it's been blended With my soul.
I Have golden ink within my pen

LIFE BY DEATH
(MY HEART IS A TITLE WAVE)

My heart beats there
There on the bed
The hands are frail, so small and red
A jumpsuit of blue
Blue for a boy.
Thus, I wonder
Will those little hands see the world ahead?
To hold the first toy?
My heart is a title wave
Rushing to break ashore.

Everything's mechanical now
I visit -leave, visit-leave...
No one made mention I had even had a child
I was told by MR.
Bill Because there was no mom to pay.
For that thing, that beast of burden, my downside
The down-cycle syndrome of false pleasures
Took her away.
So small there, and helpless
So sad.

What will be the color of his eyes?
What name can be placed on a dying child?
You only, look nurse, and I…
I would like to hold him as fathers do
But for that plastic.
He moves., a twitch, it must be painful
With all those holes jabbed into his skin
And when I wonder
"Will my heartbeat have a chance to begin?"
My heart is a title wave!

HAPHAZARD AND HARMONY

I wrote a closet full of sad songs
Tried to write away my blues
It only burned you deeper into my heart girl
You're a searing brand now on this fool

I poured all love into twelve strings
Tried to play you away some how
Tried scaring of the beauty, of a lovely day
Sleeping finally came, yet you never went away

My mix is haphazard and harmony
Sprinkled through with calamity
Iced over with history
Haphazard and harmony.

I walked the straight line from dust "till dawn
Tried for strength for keeping clean
It made me merely sicker of your world girl
And hard for me to get along

My mix is haphazard and harmony
Sprinkled through with calamity
Iced over with history
Haphazard and harmony

I cried an ocean full of tears
The Mississippi lined my face
This only stained what pages I wrote upon
Now my face is a desert I cannot trace

Haphazard and Harmony
Nothing is right, I will never be free
Now paradigm is my parody
Haphazard and Harmony.

BURIED DREAMS

I once had some big dreams in my sights
With a silver lining behind every image
Many nights were filled beneath darkened lights
Working toward hard-earned goals, by pencil and pen.

I set my heart to write at every chance
Filing pages with poverties, pains and fears
There were pieces of love, and rhythm for dance
And sad, sad songs for pulling out the tears

A dream to someday be the best
Trying, I put everything but music on the shelf
To make these big dreams come true
Writing forever without any rest
Weeklong hours, stressing my health

As life's mystery became the biggest clue
Hardships came and went, making originality
As I shook a little me in each step
And my, staggered far from reality

Every simple thing that glistens or gleams
Was another spade in the fold of the pit!
At the very depths bottom of my dreaming heart
Laid the goals in a hole for buried dreams

DEAD MAN'S EYES

Dead man looking through bankers' eyes
Cashed out inside, there's no disguise.
Old nurse staring through tender eyes,
Slowly rocking, waiting for her prize.
Platinum children reaching for hungry skies.
Plated ears hear not their little moans.
A marble mask defines a heart of stone.
As the beast in the dark house, tell his lies.

Death and destruction all through their years.
Refusal and rejection - their first of kin.
Taking nothing lightly, simpleness they fear.
It is a timeless trap they are in.
Closest to nobody so dear.
Their crimson filled eyes make evaporated tears!

Sweating farmer seeing through olden eyes,
A mushroom cloud slowly floating high.
A rug weaver sees a spiritual bond now
So important is one thread for her prize.
Their studies have shown it over with now.
Do you hear Natures warning cries?
The Boy Scout promised sincerely how
God heard his blood in the trench when it died.

Death and destruction, all through their years,
Refusal and rejection their kin,
Taking nothing rightly, simpleness they fear,
It's a timeless trap you're in.
A ruling house staring through dead man's eyes,
Hearing no blood when it cries.

GUITAR

Amidst the still air of the mourning
Crescent dark nights gone by
With a thunderous booming adjoining
The shrill of its roving cry

Scream, scream aloud, MY fretted friend
Whale to your utmost desire
So many souls tied and embedded
Into your silvery wires

Your visage encages so much passion,
Uncountable they go, eclipsed by your smashin'
Sound becomes from your presence
Raging or pleasant and mellow

I grab you and laps into hours
Of bar chords major and minor.
Starlet to relinquish their power
Coursing through your bodies uncountable

Essences bleed through your silvery strings
Your spell pumping through silvery veins
The heart's a knot tied to the guitar.
Entangled with strings.

EARLY MORNING MERRY MELODIES

Early morning merry melodies
A toucan glass of wine
A migraine from the night before
To make the ole teeth grind

I have searched in a thousand bottles
Ran along the sands of time
For something to fill an emptiness
But there was nothing I could find

Roamed along desert streets at night
Wasted and blown my mind
Searching along an empty world
It's hard to see when your blind

Early morning merry melodies
A toucan glass of wine
A migraine from the night before
To make my young teeth grind

It's a wonder I ever got this far,
Can't even swim but dive
At rest on my head in toppled cars.
Do humans have nine lives?

There is an answer, but it is not mine...
No more merry melodies
My atoms are over ionized
Emptiness is a history

Early morning merry melodies
A glass of cool aid is now divine
A migraine once is no more
I finish up with my nine to five.
©August 5, 1992

LIVING LIFE IN LETTERS

Time is nipping at midnight
It is I once again,
Exercising my love through the pen.
These pages that I scribe,
Carry out my life
Living life in letters once again.

Morning has just become,
Clock hands begin approaching one.
The day will start with "How I love you,
How have you been?

Here am I, inside these lines.
A heart attempting to define,
All the love I hold for you
The world of poets cannot describe,
A life relying on the power of the pen.

With working out every word,
Once complete and heard,
You should feel my spirit
In the pages in your hand.

I am so sad that this is so,
However, feel the need to let you know,
How much I love you down within,
My love is stronger than the power of the pen".

Another day is fit to start
As I finish pouring out my heart
Without from within.
These pages here are me,
Exerting my sympathy,
Cause I know, I am responsible...
For tearing you apart.

Now living life in letters
I bid you, "Hug me as I am,
Hold me close to your heart
Dearest Mother.
Be these only pages, they are me
All I have, to give
Living life in letters once again".

© May 9-1992
Author: JIMMY LOWE
All Rights Reserved.

HOW

When I reach the top to cross the bridge
To be the walls of precious stone,
To reach the mountains tallest ridge;
How high must my knees take the bone?

Like tumbleweeds with no control,
Shuffle on grains of rubble,
Through deserts tiring role
How often to go far, and stumble!

Instead of broken by oak; and dim,
Where lights ray shines bright
On the edge of the forest.
How long will I search for delight?

A swirling whirlpool within,
Still as a casket without;
To reach the bottom of this endless lake
How many dives will one have to take?

THESE FRIGID WALLS

These frigid walls no teardrop torn
Years throughout my stay.
The born to be deceived,
Fill her halls. She is the beast
Your spirit to slowly decay.
Buildings of block, a backdrop of laws
To govern who give their lives
That she may reach a height beyond her cause.
Help no more defines my hell
As if man's hand did ever.
Well, she meant, one time I'm sure
In all her tactics clever.
Instead, her evils all befell,
My heart, my mind, my soul,
Left here forever days or dead:
Freed or face her clay.
These frigid walls no teardrop shed
Hard heartbeat breathing
For change is bound, aim is well;
But she was made to take to hell.
To the chair, so many she sent.
From without so good she seems,
Until inside her head, you're locked
The robber of life and dreams.
"'Here! Taste my ale ", she'll say.
"But do not return ", knowing she is mocked.
So sure, you have her beat...
Her weight up off your chest.
Like the jest catches in unawares,
You're captured by her constant stare.
In her beam, she screams, "You will be there".
These frigid walls
This Hell
Known only by her heart...
Those for her.......whom fell.

BURNING UP MY VOICE

Burning up my voice
Trashing a small piece with each crumpled package
My tenor has grown horse
Take a toke, gag, and choke
Speaking through the wreckage

Who had what it takes,
A barrel bass to a hair-splitting tenor
That's the breaks
A deceitful heart
Washed it all from the eyes glimmer

Burning up my voice
In a fog bitten haze, blurry bent mind
God forbid choice
When it is one to ware, warp,
And leave confined

Burning up my voice
Had what it takes
God forbid choice
That's the breaks
Burning up my voice.

© April 1-1994
JIMMY LOWE

LONG GOODBYES-CHEAP TOBACCO

A purple sky setting on yellow waters
The shadow of a bird from way up high
Two silhouette figures, voices crackling
To a prow piece, in slow rhythm with a tide

As the entire world is jumping, in mass confusion
Everything runs past their eyes
They see no red leaves diving, off the maples
Or the gray blanket up above harming lives

Cheap fuel smelling like rotten apples
A little squeeze of the hands and she cries
The coffer in his heart is nailed and stapled
A grave love, the scene is forever in his mind

Long good-byes, cheap tobacco, and cloudy eyes
He is the true actor, pretending all is normal
While he has been shipwrecked down inside.
Long good-byes and cheap tobacco since he died.

MARRIED TO MISERY

Half full-on a bar stool
Holding my wife in my hand
Burning out memories of yesterday
Who here does not understand?
Nothing in life is forever, in love we delight
When I came home one evening
To find true love had said good-bye

So, I sit now in this bar room
By chains invisible
Anchored to my bottle And memories of her.
Who here could know just how I feel?
When I say, "I can't lay her down"
A king may have some precious jewels
But the shoot glass is my crown
I'm married to misery, and I can't lay her down

Sit me a sail whiskey ocean
The only plot where I feel sound
The King will have his precious jewels
But that shot glass is my crown
I'm married to misery
And I can't lay her down.
(Refrain after last verse)

To have this ornament I traded,
A star of Hollywood.
I sail Whiskey Ocean to Sadness Island
The only plot where I feel good
Yeah, to my bottle, I do the wed
And vow her each night to be empty
Before I fade out for bed

Whiskey Ocean set my sail for Sadness Island
The only plot where I feel sound
The king has many precious jewels
But this shoot glass is my crown
I am married to misery
And I cannot lay her down

© 1982
JIMMY LOWE

REGULAR

Too old to tumble, too young to die
Starting to mumble, I don't know why
There never giving up, never giving in
Always there to help a struggling friend.

Walk with me down fifth tier. Tell me what makes
The pain you hear. Cold as Custer! Heaven's sakes.
He has a family who loves him so.
Hoping for liberty, when can he go?

He will stomach the sweat and feces all year long.
Awake to the sting of a buzzers gong.
His meals resemble a buzzard's feast.
While the public think its heaven, so they yeast, yeast…

"Take their recreation, what chance for degree.
We'll take it to the congress and plea, plea, plea".
So, what about those with a future in life?
Still, they carve the back with a journals knife.

I'm too old to tumble, too young to die.
I'm starting to mumble; I don't know why.
I'm never giving up, never giving in,
Fighting' fire with water, Fighting' pen with Pen.

NICE SHORT RIDE

It will take a nice short ride
To get me over you.
All the exercises I have tried
Still hasn't pulled me through.
It will take a nice short ride
To set my heart at ease
A nice short ride
Whatever I do.

How many things have I tried?
Lawdy, I have not a clue.
The creek runs reminiscence outside
My face is covered with dew.
On my forehead, you lied,
To set my mind at ease.
It'll take a nice short ride
Before we are through.

While you sit in milk and honey baby
I am frostbitten rent
It sure was not too hard my lady
To get all my money spent.
From luxury to card board I went.
My future was marred
Cause you were my star.
I hope you took time to repent.

It will take a nice short ride
To get me over you.
All the yoga exercises I have tried
Leaves me still covered in dues.
I'll take a nice short cruise
To set my heart at ease
A nice short ride
Whatever I do

TRUE COLORS

Have you seen the such before?
Who speak of love and war?
Those who speak of Jesus Christ:
While upon the churches floor:
There are outward signs of working:
Signs identical to His lure.
As to that of the man a' next,
Giving visual praise.
Sing along as the piano plays.
But deep inside is sore and vexed.
Once a week the spirit flexed.
Pumped up, I'm sure.
But amidst such human wrecks
Are alighted, then deplored.
This is not the way
For what we owe: to repay
Praising God today,
Then serving hell tomorrow.
Once headed through the door,
The spirit quenched and darkened,
Flinches to restore
Upon some men's chest:
True colors go two ways,
Those of our Lord,
Or those astray.
What will it be?
Wake up world;
Mansions in the heavens,
Or shipped wrecked?

© MAY 1992 JIMMY LOWE

MITE BREAD AND BUG SOUP

Ashes in my bread
Bugs are in my soup
I cannot say what kind it was
Now I know it is just bug soup

Dirt is on my mites
Mites are on my bread
They tried to say its corn
Looking' more like mite bread

Mite bread
Bug soup
Ashes in my bread
Mite bread - bug soup

A bend is in y screw
That screw's inside my head
Don't make it turn whatever you do
Mite bread, bug soup, bent screw

Matches in my vest
My vesture is on you
I guess you know the rest
You are bent too

Come home one night
Home came to me
Oblivious to, history
Soup on the stove cooked and cold
I warmed them up and ate them whole

Ashes in my bugs
Bugs were in my soup
I can't recall what kind it was
Tasted kind 'a like - Bug soup

Mite bread
Bug soup
My match is you
Bent screw

CAN NOT SEE THE SUNSET

Can not see the sunset any more
Just the shadows of its life upon the floor
Or glimpse a little of its rays
Bouncing off a wire across the way
I cannot see the sunset any more

I cannot see the stars, a way up high
Neither dippers, nor the moon passing by
Maybe a fallen wish, shooting
I see nothing now but dream upon
I cannot see the sunset any more

I can see a lot of trees
Through the bars and glass and screen
But cannot turn to touch a leaf
Before it reaches old earth's floor
Cause I don't have my freedom any more

Breathing air from the man before me
Lay and dream sometimes till four
The shoes I have were worn before me
But I can't set to wondering any more
I cannot see the sunset anymore.

© JUNE 1992
JIMMY LOWE

MUSIC IS IN THE EAR OF THE BEHOLDER

There is music in the motors, all around me that whine
There is music in the yarns, when my neighbor starts to pine
There is music in the water; there is music in my words
There's music in the cows bellowing, music made by birds

There is music in the door slam, as you headed out for town
There is music in the dirt clods, upon my sweat beat brow
There's a tune in my morning oats, when they plurp-plurp to boil
Music moans from the tractors plow, you used to scratch my soil

Music in the morning NEWS, tossed by Paper Jimmy Brown
Music in the boom, of my coffee spoon, in my mind running 'round
There is music in the mountain breeze, whispered trees of Smokey Hills
There was music in the moment, that you said you love me still

Music in your heartbeat and it pounds my spirit still
There is music in the day you went away, leaving me with only bills
Even if it is sad and sorrowful, it is music that is for sure
Music in my teardrops when the splattered on the floor

Also, music in the judge's hammer, hard as that may seem
There is rhythm in my words, no matter what I write
Rhythm in that paper you used to defecate my life
It's only true that life with you, was a nightmare not a dream

CRACK MACARONI AND CHEESE

Crack macaroni and cheese
Pasta is all you can eat
When you're smoking sick
Never able to meet your needs

Trading love, home and life, then trick
Tread your family into the murky dirt
As you take a toke, gag and choke
Hooked and burning, brain cells away

The scum of the earth, for what it is worth
The man who pushes drugs for pay
By greed, he's sick, wallet so thick
Not caring what young life he wreath

Never able to meet any needs
When you burn that crystal pipe It's,
"Pass the pasta please".
Yeah, crack macaroni and cheese.

WHAT'S OWED

Girl, you had me once
Then you loved me nice
Then you ran me through with a tongue of ice

So, you called me baby
And you called me honey
Then you called divorce and took all my money

So, well, I was used once
But it doesn't happen twice
While you taught me well, well isn't that nice

Somebody's coming' baby
Headed your way
He has an ice sickle heart and ready to play

Because your karma is spread
Your seeds are sown
How well will you take it when you get what's owed?

MY WORLD

When another day is through
To find Mr. Sunshine low
I'm headed back to my lonely bed
Into another world I go

I have many good friends
Their all happy for me
If they hang around, all depends
On how I want them to be

When a weekend roll's around
Or I just feel blue again
I just take my tablet down
And visit some old friend

It is my little lonely world
Made of paper and pen
I can at any time come out
But you can never come

To my little lonely world
Of paper and pen
Take a tablet down
I am there again.

A THOUSAND FLAT TIRES

(Hell) "Get up! You have a call."
"You look so good, there in the grass
As the wind does blow.
I have been waiting for some years for a visit...
There is a strange, sad look on your face
Son! What is it?
How's your mother, brothers and my best friend?
Quick! Tell me now, because you can't come again.
That you loved me son, your face, men don't cry.
Isn't that a beautiful sky?"

"Hey old man, wherever you are...
I would have come sooner,
But had a thousand flat tires.
I'm grown now. I turned twenty-one in prison.
I see you from time to time in dreams vision.
Things are not the same since you went away,
We still stayed drunk, but our skies are not gray.
I do not understand why you did all you did...
Whip, curse, and abuse your own kids."

"This is a nice piece of ground, except the noise.
I watch in hysteria young girls, silly boys
Cross the street, living so dangerous.
I hope you're not so careless and not using dope.
It is cold here, awaiting my doom.
I find no one, kind or groom: Roots and clay for all I have done.
I've been thinking, has it really been so long?"

"I thought I'd visit, verily, one time.
It was the tightest day of my life, the crime
That took you away. No men are not supposed to cry...
That old tree sure has grown since I first came by.
I forgive you old man, for what it's worth.
And stop to tell you, God lifted your curse.
I cannot remember saying before yah left the skies blue,
So, I stopped to let you know that: I did love you".

© MARCH 11-1993
AUTHOR: JIMMY LOWE

COP A SQUAT

Cop-a-squat-n-sit a lot
Ease your weary bones
I have a tale you, may sadden to hear
But it can only be told in tones.
Take a toke, gag-n-choke
Blow your reason away.
It could appease your heart, to read my note.
Just out for a party that day.

Met a man in fashion style.
I was really stoned.
Hardily we laughed very loud: offered me a beer.
(Guess no one likes to drink alone)
Took a seat-n-watched the city smoke
As it spiraled away.
His laughter ceased when his cheeks were soaked.
Like a cut rope, he frayed!

"You're a lot like someone I used to know,
Who had sought advice on how to fair?
After giving names to the law, I guess from fear.
He did what I would never do.
Humbly he asked what to do!
To scare! I said, ""I'd shoot myself, if ever I snitched.""
On the next day, he lay, there in the ditch."
Just a kid as I was though, I missed the catch.

Cop-a-squat-n-sit a lot.
This tale is no pun.
But it never would play now for fun.
And I realized
From the waves in his eyes
That the stranger there spoke of his son!

BORN CRAZY?

Who can push you crazy?
They say it's all in your head!
Could it' a been Mr. Maybe?
Could it' a been those dying daisies,
Growing on a bed?

"Surely', they say, "It's all in your head".
Others would say that you're born that way,
But I think we're driven there instead.
Cause a wind cannot blow without motive.
Society is an excellent loco method.

Could the Doctor have dropped me on my head?
Could it have been my nurse?
No! NO! Any fine babe,
Who was made that way!
Surely could not be a curse.

Whose gonna push you crazy?
Could it be just the flick of a switch?
If it's all in my head:
Then I was as a kid.
It might have been the gin, drinking son-of-a-bitch.

Well! Well! Then I must be crazy.
Either way, I qualify for the range.
Society spends up your brain.
And when the buck is history
You don't even get back some change.

They say it's all in your head
Then I must' a been born with a burnt-out clutch.
Cause Mr. Maybe, was already over the edge.
Whose gonna push me crazy?
Will you go ask the daisy?

ROMANCING THE MICROPHONE

So, there you are
In your fantasies
A Super Star
With an upstanding stage degree.
You still don't find who you are
Playing the part
Making music, making history.

So, there you are
As clear as a tone
You see the lands
Your passport is the microphone.
Forever blind
Can't you see the brand?
Stoned for your fans
Woe betides he, who is alone.

I have once heard
It's lonely on the top
Remember Hank,
Think about the King, and Scott.
Who lost their minds!
Their best friend was a drink
They all understood
It may be good, but it is lonely on the top.

On waters front
Moments of fear
On a desert stump
Strange are the places where miracles appear.
You were left behind
In your glass of trump
What you want
Cannot be had, so you're stranded there.

They say, "It is lonely on the top", and it is true
But who wants to stop before their through?
Held up in the snow well
Waiting at the Hotel for the crew
Woe betides he who is alone
Woe betides he who is alone
The cost of romancing the microphone.

BEAUTY OF THE STORM

Sometimes when we hold out
Through what storms life delivers,
When there seems as if no hope exists.
Whatsoever, wherever, awhile...
All along, we're wrong,
As hope supersedes. We want
To see those storms as raining down
On our parade. And fail to see its beauty,
Allowing dark clouds to push this away
From our minds. We hope
For sunny skies, and miss the beauty
Of the falling rain. We see the ugliness
In our hearts, it pours out so easily
In the storms. Don't look for scary lightning,
Or the *simulated* ugliness of death:
As Peter, we take our eyes away from Christ,
And right off, we're in, deeper than
Before we hit rock bottom; to let our heart span
To stone. The devil, by Jesus Christ,
Must run, must flee!
So, keep your eye upon
The beauty of the storm, Jesus Christ.

RUNAWAY AND THE SILVER TONGUE STRANGER

Whoever came up to be knocked down?
Kicked, cursed, unloved, and slapped around?
To find the street as an abused child
By families falling out, left behind, cold and wild
Night after night to heavy metal music sounds.

The silver tongue has no remorse
Twist on young minds, with an easy subtle force.
Needing some attention, runaways will dotingly tag along
A bent bridled horse, dancing to the pied pipers' song
Runaway, that way does not have to be

In an arcade excepting broken hearts
You play the games, parlay to play the part
Anything to take away the pain
Beginning the life of a loser when the stranger imparts
The silver tongue likes the lives undone

The mind begins wondering, hardly pondering
Anything to take away the pain
So, you look for seclusion in a state of mass confusion
While you're dancing to the tune that the old piper plays
Reaching for the moon at noon, at day, from the gutters where you lay.

ROCK LEGENDS

So many contributions
History has made
All the mass confusion
Wherever it was played
Riots in the street, to be at feet
Upon the stage

To many it is a big dream
Lights in all a glare
I'll be another rock-n-rolling king
To Hendrix I will compare
Study every night to make it right
Working for a wage

Many hated that rock music
Said, "Take it off the air"
But legends never die
There is music everywhere
Rock-n-roll survives from dedicated lives
Even in New Age

It's no modern misconception
Rock is a disease
Truly an infection
Only the truth if you please
When they saw their hand turn green
They began to turn the page

So many contributions
Stoners have all made
Roll on intuition
Great legends never fade
Practice all year long, for the perfect song
Ageing on the stage.

STRANGER IN YOU

Four people in the ocean of my mind.
It is just so tiring to stay afloat.
One would have me wondering,
So, the other may chastise.
"You've blown it now. You deserve no love".
And another wonders'; just how who went wrong?
Personality, a puppy cuddly warm.
Attitude, A raving bear in wet paper chains.
Wisdom is experiencing that money cannot buy
Sanity is balanced on the point of my pen lines.
It is not so confusing if the scales of death are known.
Their alive inside of you after their gone.
Four people existing here, inside my head.
Oh, what terrible things they can quote.
Prime objective of one is to maim and hate.
Another's best ally is love.
Pushing the insides from state to state.
Like a hurricane kicking a dove.
As another other, finds favor in musical notes.
My mind is full of plenty.
My heart full of wants to do good.
My spirit reaching out for peaceful Eternity;
From a flesh of rock, water and wood.
Worm logged, these hands that write will someday be.
My heart will rot into stick and stone
However, this hearts spirit has eternal love.
It is so concrete to be understood.
I have done the waltz on lacerating lions.
Preferring to walk with Lazarus and Lamb.
Who can tell a man his company to keep?
I watched pythons, pirates and priest.
Even walked asleep in my wake;
In haunting jungles, a time or two.
The same strangers in me are strangers in you.

Familiar strangers in the ocean of my mind.
Familiar strangers in you.

© 1-16-1995

MR. DEATH

You may think him kind of reverie
A pestilence to some degree
Or having chutzpah, spit in his face.
Puling words of the validness
Of the lanky state feared to caress,
Have no piquant stories told!

No paltry haggle teeming
Of his crassly esteeming,
Ubiquitous hoary rift,
Will return the Spryling to his youth.
Dank faces whine effusive
Crying out "He is abusive".
Affront the pale rift.

He is not sensuous or paltry,
Lucrative, nor sees confetti
He is ahead, he is arrear
Everlasting lifeless peer
Stands off ground, and some day here.
Un-trivial I stand ready.

Unpiquant Spryling teeming.
No pulina yet esteeming
Mr. Death for what he can be.
And our comfort is only
Our worse dreaming
Or an ever-present pleasantry.

AGE IN YOUTH

In the wrinkled substitution
Of these features called my face
There is a process of the ages taking place.
They say I looked a little younger
With less numbers in the race.
Does anybody think that sounded strange?

In the marrow of the knuckles
That never looked so out of place
There is a glimmer of the aging taking place.
They say less eaten, even today
Puts more depth around the waist
Wouldn't one think it is time to change?

By the mirror contribution
All my creases haunt me now.
I know it as just illusion
Putting more worries on my brow.
Guess I'll still get by somehow.
As the magnitude of time must yet catch me!

From the multiple discretions
Inside the tombstone called my heart
The youth and all these lines do not agree
I know that I should act, more my age;
But old was I, when I was but three.
So now have youth, I never had the chance to be.

In ado concentration
With these thoughts, they call my brain,
There is a process of the aging taking change.
They say that this fool is no dummy.
But the eyes cop out to what is insane.
Goes to show how much they really mind

When the withered resolution
In the reverb of my ears
Has the process of agelessness among my peers;
They say they're a little stronger.
Yet show the same pattern as past years.
Do you think they thought they could escape the grid?

How about the sensuous?
Selling dreams across the wire
Saying special things, the blind desire.
Feeding on their hunger
(One is mange the other is mire)
Do think it pertains to one we know?

What a high price on commission
When municipal eyes are green.
"Now there's a process of the ages to be seen"
If that's a heart, power offers?
Then my preference is to remain green
Though I'm on the Big Stage, I will be some regular Joe.

From the featured substitution
Of these wrinkles called my face,
I see processes of the ages in the race.
They say science made them stronger;
Yet I failed to see the smoothness in its face.
Can anybody deny me this truth?

In the marrow of these knuckles,
History can be traced
To the ancient futures pace.
They say it can't go on much longer,
Because we're running out of space.
Should we not press onward in our aging youth?

CANNOT KNOW A PRODUCT (BY THE PITCH OF ITS SALE)

I thought that I had learned women
When I was young;
But I only eluded myself.
Before I saw the happenings,
My heart was on the run.
And I was next to fearing for health.

You cannot know a book by the cover.
Can't use a title to tell a tale,
Cannot know a product
By the pitch of its sale.
You cannot say a woman loves
Just because she's a lover.

Met her through a friend.
Knew right off that we were meant to be.
We made love, as I fell
I would carry her forever.
If that so willed, she,
Till my back broke her thread.

Quilted one day with sleep
My eyes found not my lover:
For a biker friend of mine.
So, I learned about the words we live to,
And thought women were easily knew.

But you cannot know a book by the cover.
Cannot use a title to tell a tale
Cannot know a product
By the pitch of the sale.
You cannot say a woman loves
Just because she is a lover.

SPELLBOUND BY MY MUST

By the twilight of moonbeam
One to shun, one to share
One drunken dumb, none to care
She held my hand in dream.
For this stock she would dare.

"Come closer here", cried she,
In her pulsating want to grasp
Wanting to feel all I am.
My heart cumbered to plunder
As she begged to take me in.

From the drunken rose a stir
Thought I sunken right then
Laughing at our face's sheepish grins.
With but snores form her boyfriend's blur
I was welcomed into her, den.

A second not to lose
Passions hotly brewed
Engaging in her favor
No want was, but to please her.
While knowing her to be so crude.

In the fever of our lust
With no heart about true love;
My needs gave her my shove.
Flirting hard with danger, I was,
Spellbound by my must!

A shark in her snare,
Therefore, the sucker I just played
Action for which I later paid.
I found no tokens there,
I often wonder how
I allowed it to be this way?

Slowness just was not her,
Quickly made way deeper inside
But the lust in her eyes could not lie.
For anything, ready she was
In her eyes was nothing but parties and balls.

I saw through her vest
Despite the swelling in my chest,
And dumped her in my hating,
When her eyes stopped raising my zest.
Normal as the world, she was an anapest.

UNETHICAL DEED

Their weapon, the unethical deed:
Dubbed to stab yet make not bleed.
The point? The piercing! What has been done.
A conduct of the uncanny one.

A wound not salve, nor pill can heal.
No friendship can bandage an ordeal.
For the deed thrust, pierces what bends.
An affliction struck at moral kind.

When kindness rips deeper than steel
Termed as weakness, because you feel;
The nice guy; who gave a Bro slack,
Stabbed with a smile in the back.

IN THE BLISTER BURNING BLUE

Calmly, trickled the tired cool creek
Over shiny stones, under shaky stem
Of grassy weeds, downward water will seek.

In the blue of blister burning day
Youth in masculine, longing to swim,
No pool! Just a cool creek and a way.

Engineering mud for home a made pool.
A dawn secured good and strong,
By afternoon to reach the goal.

Once work and school through
Swimming their fill for summers long
In the day of blister burning.

REQUIESCAT

No repertoire has he for claim
Renitent of poseur games
Mental mode relax-and contemplate
As adult children play

That not with toys as girls and boys
But with the mind, they try their pith
Excessive loud noise, anti-practical poise
Yet imbalanced and lithe

Like wolf hounds a' prey, animals' parlay
Against the weaker, their weapon is time
In their powering pith, their tongue dug ditch
Their mere mortal soul shall lay.

THE SANDS OF NOUNS

No army's valor have I led to victory
No chariots where soldiers combat fate
Some of none, jewels for to fence
No treasures of gold nor frankincense

No colonial appareled throne
Nor chose a lot to acquire my power
No tuxedos, tied, nor alligator shoes
No majors upon the business hours.

But I have fought hard, old poverty
And rode the radio days stalking skies,
Or sober southern suns
Rode rowdy wrangler whirlwinds miles high in eminence.

Saw the peaceful day from mounds of stone
Felt gentle breezes stroll across the face of flowers
Walked lighted deserts late at night
The sage forest in lifeless presence

No expeditions across the sky
Studied the dippers form points on high
Trespassing stars in quest for life
Shooting stars cradled in my love's eyes.

Saw great master pieces stand
In the castle of cloud
I have done nothing, and all, then and now
Standing tall on the sands of nouns.

A WORKING BOYS CHRISTMAS

Their eyes lit up like candles
When toys came through the door
Beholding all the new things
They had never seen before.
Eight little eyes jumping with glee
Adoring all the pretty colors;
That one's for you, this one for him
And that one, this is me.

Summers were a workshop.
Each winter beat the breeze.
Sleds full of wood from the mountains
In a snow up to their knees.
Mammas mighty strength from The Fountain
Just boys at work till their fingers bleed or freeze,
Stayed baby brothers kept warm.
The plows of poverty are hands like these.

So many countless faces of strangers
To children like these, appear now as angels.
Mamma read from the Holy Bible
Jacobs's ladder and fruits on a tree.
Joy is ever in those strange faces
The love of the Lord kept baby brothers warm
That is what Christmas means to me.

Schoolhouses changed like clouds
By road maps learning to read.
Signs of times as poor kids in town
Bussed away from high society
Christmas carols: Moses and Pharos
Jacob's stairwell to eternity.
Once a year came love in barrels
That is what Christmas means to me.

ON MY JOURNEY BACK

Staring out the window
Waiting for the rain.
Cool fresh summers wind blow.
Patiently going insane.

Bright bolts threaten everywhere.
The darkened sky complains.
The forest trees all whisper there,
"That must be so--- much pain."

The singing birds don't all disappear.
Storm in the heavenly air.
A little house blows in the wind,
Some life is looking there.

Ciphering came those little lives.
The water says beware.
But those little birds must fill the sky
Singing, "Rain on! I soar!"

But when the gloom of murky night
Turn the waters to a pitchy black,
Then the flickering reflecting lights
Dance on his rolling back.

Floating out the window in the rain
In a blues attack.
Patiently going insane.
Or am I... On my journey back?

All I read and see
Suggest running but watching every step.
All of God, indeed!
Unending Help.
Crackling, caring, staring
Out the window at the rain
Working a way back home to the sea
On my journey back.

DESERTED AGAIN

Deserted again, my face to the wall
Nobody to hold these hands, No lady
To wake up to; or fruitful dog to sniffing jeans.
No lover to pitch-bitch when I am late.
No body to hold my hand. No Lady!
Come screaming world, sound right now.
No lover to pitch-bitch when I'm late.
Even a woman to slap my face and shout jealousies.
Even screaming would seem like loving right now.
Everything about freedom is kicking me down.
Just a woman to slap my face and shout jealousies.
Her waste of honest money would even be nice.
Everything about freedom wants to kick me down
An evening about, beneath a midnight sun.
A waste of honest money could even be pleasing.
The lull of traffic when I am in my hurries.
An evening beneath a midnight sun.
Standing by the shores of Twilight Sea.
The lull of traffic when I am in my hurries.
Talking at dinner tables with family.
Standing by the shores of seas.
Neighbors shouting while there at home.
Talking at the dinner table with family.
A flat tire or being stuck in the mud.
Neighbors shouting while they're at home.
A cool tall glass of ice water.
A flat tire or being stuck in the mud.
Brothers borrowing tools and moving away.
A cool tall glass of ice water.
Waiting, hot and tired, to cash a payroll check.
Brothers borrowing tools then moving away.
Shopping for weekly supplies of grub.
Waiting hot and tired, to cash a payroll check.
Yard sales, swap meets, fishing and finding pennies.

Shopping for weekly supplies of grub.
Deserted again, I sit with my face to the wall.
Yard sales, swap meets, fishing and finding pennies.
Everything about freedom is kicking me down.
No body to hold my hand. No Lady!
Deserted again, a' sit with my back to the wall.

ANTI...

I don't like football, I'm anti sports man
Don't study sitcoms, anti-television
I don't purchase papers, I'm antiwar
So, it seems that's all they're written for

I'm anti hate, anti-greed, anti-heroin
Anti-speed. I'm anti fear, anti-luck, anti-dog and anti-duck
Anti-ignorance, anti-blame. You pull the trigger
Another takes the blame.

I don't hate women, I'm against rape
Got tired of drugs doing me, I'm anti dope.
God bless the children, I'm anti perversion
It seems the entire world is made of intrusion.

No gold and silver, I'm anti jewels
Less evil communications, I'm anti fools.
Anti-fight, anti-kill, antiabortion, I don't like pills
Baby you can't make children if you're not digging for thrills.

Anti-hate, anti-greed, anti-heroin, anti-speed
I'm anti fear, anti-luck, anti-dog and anti-duck
Anti-ignorance, anti-blame. You pull the trigger
A neighbor takes the blame.

IF ONLY I, WERE YOU

If only I, were you
You had to sit here this a-way
Just think of all the splendid things you could do
Then you would admit how wrong you really are
To condemn the condemned behind these walls of grey

If only I, were you
The man who sits and makes the rule
Just think of all the things I could do
Capriciously submit, how wrong you are
From within your glass house of pots and clay

When the walls start, all to falling'
The panes shatter your windowed eyes
Who then can you call to donate some cash?
When hell is raining down in acid flame
Whom will you call to complain?

Your pots of clay have run empty
You don't see all around you crying.
Ran the cup of oil dry for your light
While I have enough light to see your eyes
Light from my God in the sky.

If only I, were you
While you had to fit in this way
I know exactly what you would do
You would slit your wrist, Democratized
From within your menial mind, beside your pots of clay.

CRAZY EDDIE

Once I lived with crazy Eddie
The ooooooh-riginal one.
Yes, I lived with crazy Eddie
Not so slow to speak,
Picking his teeth,
On a shotgun.

Eddie was a warrior in his day.
Life on the limb is not the only way.
By the hands of fate, what cards he drew.
Forever awaiting nothing, nothing to do.
Give him a token for just a time.
In return for a complaint, he is ogre and mime
Checking' out the dances, his right to see.
His dream of romances now takes him by the jeans.

Crazy Eddie, you cannot undo all that is done
Life is rough, difficult and steady
Left without love
All alone is no fun
Come a red moon will we be ready
Eddie For the Son?

Eddie! Crazy Eddie!
When I lived with Crazy Eddie
The only, lonely one
Yes, I lived with Crazy Eddie
Took down by the street.
Likes to preach,
The cold blue gun.

JUST LET IT GO

I never said one grey word,
Just calmly walked away
However, stood first watching
Still seeing the crazed look of her eye,
Her untamed hair, pulled behind the ear,
The house and remember my age.

It took place in the kitchen
Not more than twelve was I,
She was not preparing chicken,
But her precious self to die.
I could not scream or panic:
But by strength, calmly walked to her side.

Her scarlet rose gushing, gushing, gushing.
From the floor, I cast my gaze
To the flicker of the bright shiny blade
Sinking into her fair white skin:
Once, twice, three and again.
What does a ten-year-old say?
To see his mother acting this way!

What does an adult say?
To such a scene come flickering?
An old eight-millimeter film forever
On constant, scratchy, soundless replay...saying:
"Just let it go, just let it go".
While the scene plays on in the backdrop of a mind.

STAIRWELL TO YOUR CONSCIENCE

I have no jewels to bequeath
Or some unknown bank account
All I have are stories and relief
From time trolling in great amount
I cannot tell them all in truth
Or all completely lies
Nor vintage you with youth
Or stimulate your pride

For every earnest story, each may know
Contains a bit of writing that's a quite bit real
To push a plot into its flow
By liquid point of steel
To pin your minds unto my page
Relax, be free from every care
As I begin to set some stage
You've now one foot on the stairs
Get off, if warning dares
But carefully, not so abrupt.

Ah, but there is an uncaught catch
You have both now fitted well
But how many steps were skipped? Fetch
Your conscience, it is the only way to tell
Look into your own minds mirror!
Where have you sojourned
Did you step so high you fear too, so?
Or low you must be scared
So, think not to travel onward
"You've no need for contemplation?"
Where you have just gone
Would you be there?
With no inclination?

Step Two: Your minds mirror
Which was withal in mention!
Does the image dull, or gently glow?
Would you wonder here of sentient?
Oh! Close your eyes and place yourself
Get your unconscious off the shelf
Where with it would you go?
It is just a mental maze,
Through pain, or Rome or snow;
Or the dagger to dog its own good health
As your past depicts the faze.

The time has come for C
As we did gender A and B
Unlike two first; but we
Be not careless with three
Steps one and two were your own
Now you walk the third with me
To finish merely you may find
What lies inside to wonder at now?
The prism of your mind!

No pendent pedant pendant
Permits powers for your propensity
To persuade parallel perception
Per, pre-purposed presentation
To peek and peer through the mind's porthole
Proceed precisely, do not prod
For all you are provoking
Is peace before you nod.

Now step onto your stairway
For I've taken you through your tale
Of which you, the character
A ride through your mind you have hitched.
Now, say "Fare-de-well",
While you have not moved an inch.

TITLE TO MY TALE

I searched a world I never knew
For a title to my tale
Digging beneath rocks and kicking over stone
Whenever one was there
I acted the jest and 'woke alone
Bleeding for one so true
But never felt the blood in my bones
'Till I first saw you

I've kicked the dogs and cursed the cats
But age has taught to still, be kind
No more lumberjack, or breaking my back
To put money in my hand
Placing a ring upon your hand
And canny this worldwide spat
Through a thousand muds for a life with you

My search now over, I found my one
You're the title to my every tale
Now feeling so at ease, it is wonderful
At the thought of you I never pale
I am forgetting fear and my woes
Emotions of love storm like al
 You're the title to my tale.

CHANGES IN YOU

I see no vehicles racing about
No children playing in the arts
No pretty women in the finest dress
 I guess I'm just not at the park.

You can only write what you can see
It is rigid to write anything else
I see a thousand men in line with me
Waiting for tomorrows.
A thousand men in line each day
Whose laughter drowns their sorrows!

I am not looking at neon lights
Or heights of greenly rolling hills
Musty cities, dingy streets; But that's alright
I will awake, if God wills, embracing all my horrors.

I cannot watch humble weeds tumble
Or blinding dust from hard winds blow
I can't even see the length of an arrow
But who must listen to what I know?
Just another caged up sparrow.

What do you write when you cannot see?
Beyond the limits of living hell
In a dank and drowsy cell
You can only write what you can see.

I see the world is changing
Through the eyes of their paper
NEWS Just as all men must one day do!
I'll jot down changes I've went through.
I will jot down changes in you.

LITTLE BROTHER

Listen to me little brother
For I know you're just a pup
You have a long life to live
Stay free, don't ever mess it up

You may think that I am one
To be giving such advice
But I have learned in the hardest way
And the good Lord knows I'm right

So, you take heed and listen
To all these words I say
Then you will know just what to
When trouble comes your way

Watch out for the crowds
Don't ever give them slack
For they will smile to your face
As they stab you in the back

Believe me this because my eyes have seen
I know it happens all the time
When the pressure is applied
You fall for their crimes

Loyal friends are hard to come by
And seldom ever found
However, once there and when you need them
They are always around

So, remember this my brothers
The best friends I'll ever have
When Jesus Christ is beside you
Do not sweat being stabbed.

PORTABLE SANDBOX

When there, hanging out
Below the stars
Sundown talking through box guitar
Was no doubt when I bend them strings
Scratching out sounds to make the sunset ring
That I was hooked forever on the sound

"You got to get up", They say, "Get around!
Piddling strings don't appease no account".
Looking out over things that change
Scratching out bruises that the apple brings
Culture is forever turning around.

And there I stood,
Plugged into the thing
Hooked on the sound of mortal change
Hooked on the natural high it brings
In my portable sandbox
Hanging on the scaffold of strings.

A string per month
Every pebble is named
Slowly walking with an end in aim
There is no doubt; we are not just a plaything
A portable sandbox, to devise the sting
At my heart hooked, to never refrain

When there I stood, plugged into the thing
Hooked on the sound of mortal change
Hooked on the natural high it brings
In my portable sandbox
Fretting the sound of strings.

Longer hang around
The entire world is nigh
Mortal walking through a bandaged sky.
Plugged into mounts of concise range.
A portable sandbox to devise a change.
As I'm hooked forever on the sound.

BABAMERICA

Somebody must run the world,
Superpower, NATO's force!
Do you really belong there, is it your choice?
To say who fights: to say who runs?
Supply them weapons, lots of guns!
To kill each other through the voice of peace.

Peace doesn't kill! I don't know where you're from.
Bang! Bang! Take it or leave it. Mud in your eye.
The fangs of injustice...
He sure gat his teeth in ever bodies pie.

You say you're not trying to run the world;
You're just begging for votes, sounds kind' a sure,
Save the world! Save the walrus? Save the Serbs!
While the homeless Americans starve on curbs?

Take a deep breath world get ready to go
In the arms of America, all else has gone infant.
Peace doesn't kill! But someone must run the show.
Take it from a sentient, "Power is their goal...

THE FOOL ON THE LOST SEA

Such a fool have I been to walk out on your love
You were true to my heart, and I was a scuzz
I'm sorry and apologize, for my guise
To have just disappeared from your blue skies, above
Must have pained you so terribly, this wicked web wove.

On a whim, I did wonder afar form your heart
That I carelessly broken, at fault of ill mind
For my deed, all I have left of you is a rhyme
Which will keep us together for what time we're apart.
Only hope can sustain me to make a fresh start.

What word's kind tone can have your hearts love again?
What rhyme may persuade your ardor to love me?
You're the only steamer to haul me from the lost sea!
What dire price, do I owe my great friend?
I would pay twice to hold you close once again!

I don't know where to turn Sunshine, what to say, what to do,
Where to go, Why I've done what I've did to put you through the night
So, I say, I'm in pain, there is no way to explain…
All around me is green, from the tears that I rain
Because, to counteract my grief, I must jest, the fool!

NOW YOU DID IT

Now you did it, Billy is sick
Ten years old, addicted to crack
Running the street
Rouging for stash
A newborn addict who will kill for cash.

Go on and say it, Michele is no longer green
No sooner got breast than she's hitting' the mainstream
Running the street
Pleasure for stash
Crafted for pleasure, so she's trading her ass.

I got to say, it just isn't right
Drug dealers ruin, innocent children's lives
Perforated by blackness, the darkness of night.
You're only making another clone of yourself
Sitting children's choices, out of reach on a shelf.

Now you done it, Billy's sick
Not even a teen and smoking crack
A slave to pleasures
For the rest of his days
Only to grow up to make another in his way

I'm gonna say...it... just isn't fair
Young people are mad whom, burn out on their air
Transplanted from light into the valley of dark
If you don't believe just what I'm saying
Just visit any park

For dealers of all kind
Children are prey
Always looking for converts
They can lead astray
Somebody is coming, coming for you
We're determined to stop your child abuse.

Go on and play it video kicks
Down at the arcade, turning tricks Billy's buddy is so rich
Michele's daddy too mean
But the real fix is friendship, it is so easily seen.

Get off yourselves parents, get it right
Your baby's futures
Depend on your insight
I'm gonna say it, don't be so crude
Don't let somebody's future, run down the tubes.

TEMPLE OF FAME

You've been drawing' faces today lady
Of people, you will meet tomorrow, for the first time.
Trying to guess my tomorrow's feelings
While you're trying to be a temple of fame
You're making your bed in the house of pain

You said in your heart, upon today
"He'll be so happy when his friends come tomorrow
That he will not notice when I go out to play".
You forget how you are unable, from time, to borrow
You cannot live tomorrow, from the present, in such a way

What apples of knowledge have you been eating baby?
You must 'a been listening to rats in the wall
You do not see the lizards' laxing on the cottage fences
For the paper mashie birdies on your bedroom hall
Lady, you have been looking, but you cannot sense it.

I had to loan my eyes to, allot of yesterdays
Before I was able even, enough to see
Human's only biggest sins are limitations
Guess I reached my limit, when I gave you my name
Therefore, my house is no longer, your temple of fame.

NEW AGE LIVING

From microscopes to microphones
In the micro-dimensions of their minds
By the microscope of my pencil, you will find
It isn't peace the monster craves.
Living in the new age

From mycologist to psychologist
In the psychochemical heart
In my symbols here apart
The here immediate they just resist
Living with age-ologist

Living in the new age
Your neighbor is your fence
Posted in the device
Of the web all around you thence
People are your stairs, actors on a stage

From cavalier to privateer
Perceptively by their deeds.
By the plainness of my pen
You have the light to see somberness
It isn't peace the monster needs.

XUSK

Evening brisk, brush the dusk
As I lay me down for dead
Who hopes to have no fossil Xusk!
Awake me late while I bed

I see the servant saying silent prayers;
The fire breathing heathen's haughty head
Alay looking here, learning little in hours
And saw there in you the me instead

Hear the heart of happiness waving hands
Sorrowful sad, singing blues of flowers,
The pangs of the proud properties-man!
As the simple submit to the higher powers.

See the soul of search and study
Reading, Reading, Reading for hours
Digging in knowledge for sandstone towers
The stressed out look on their furrowed foreheads.

Feel the naughty nip of the naked night
What it all means I just cannot explain
While the working wheels turn in my mind
I keep searching while I find

Carrions of feces fill the Autumn air
My nostrils recoil in a daunting dread
Came in a breeze so fine and fair
Pushed back a biting air of dead

A hacking halo of smiling smokers
Snorting, snorkeling, snorers of Tokers
Riding rhythmic waves wherever
In tunes untold, tossers dance in dreams despair

An evening brisk, brush the dusk
Sleeping like a kid
May we take dreams without any tussles
Just awake me from my fossil in time to be fed…

YOU ABORT YOURSELF

Abort phalanx Baby; what have you done?
Cold hearted woman, he could 'a been our son
She could 'a been your daughter.
Now it's another payment on the page of death

You could not do without, some bodies man
Laying around never went as planned.
Afraid of a little life, you took it into your hands,
To do away with it!

Down on the corner, you got what you want;
Fifty dollars and quarters, forty-minute punt.
Then Doc says, "You're having a child"
Going crazy, you take life in your power.

Abort this baby, what have you done
Whoever pays your dollar
He's the devil too
The stain on your fingers testifies to the truth

Unborn life cannot decide, whether it wants to live or die.
And your mate teases hell, which will be fair
Every aborted baby, baby
Gonna see your soul, when your turn comes to frail.

DEATH BY LOVE

They always swore to be true to each other
And vowed, "Unto death do we part"
A marriage in blue, invited the neighbors
Locking away the puppy loves of their hearts
They swore no other, or nothing could tear them apart
In sweet harmony do began they as one
A very charming couple was she and he
While the lock bond was their son.
Joyous they were with a newborn life
As they taught walk, talk and pampered love
A regular family: son, husband and wife.
Now who knows the dangers of love, except God Above?
First there came no time for sharing
For the family supplier, work quickly turned to greed
Starting to fade like noonday, was any caring
When love turned too stale with a subtle speed.
Gone were the happy nights with love and feeling.
Soft and warm hearts became stone.
Then the nights beneath the same ceiling.
So many nights together alone.
What vows taken would be broken.
Of cherish and honor ever marriage seeks.
The heart is strange when guilt's sin sets to soaking,
When time kept growing longer, his mind slowly grew weak.
Guilt feelings of nights alone in the office
Ate at the core of his being
As if it wasn't enough… this
Drove him to do terrible and harsh crazy things.
So dearly did she love him, her loving man.
In her Ray ban grotesque eyes of the beatings
Applied makeup by scared shaky hands.
Meeting friends always with merry greetings
To cover horrible pains volcanic in her side.
There was all along a disaster brewing.

While lying awake at night she hurt and cried.
Her fear was rejecting his doing.
But fear is dangerous when it is stewing.

THE HYPOCRITE

I have been told that heaven is mixed
With stars to lie in long
To fill yourself with song
Soothing the bluest soul
You await your hold; I spotted mine

I set my goals, my eyes are fixed
Tired of the role
Played it for too long
I know that God does own my own soul
But I cannot live the weary way of the hypocrite

I'm breaking the mold, where their transfixed
Have paid their toll
And I paid it for too long
Say to God and right my wrongs
But I cannot carry on as a hypocrite.

LO, THE POET

Lo, the poet allots fame, afore gotten
Who would fall the scribe, alive still, when forgotten!
Journalist labor daily, their muck found in pails
The poets work, for virtues famous, tell the tales
So, it's been tried, words proven him immortal
Stole by life, here, in rhymes reasonable total.

Plays of passion, verses or sonnets of shame
Power of the pen, destine to or not to tame
Has no man mightier a sword, than an odd poet's quill
Touch the stars, love Aphrodite's, if one so will
Pains construct, obedient jots
Connotations fill later empty slots

Lo. The poet spent above so many a page
Ran the race to grave, recognized then as a sage
Bright minds befell emotion, trapped to tell the torn
Silk words across some pearly paper
Prick the poet's heart, these worlds, his thorn
Lo, another poet has been born.

2/24/1993

POSTAL ACCESS TO YOUR HEART

Holidays come, and holidays go

Seasons flourish well.

I must let you know

You're the water in my hell.

The soothing to my pangs

You are my smile

So, I send you my love

Across the miles.

12/15/19193

LOVE IS...

Sex is loved!
But love is not sex!
Whatever then is love?
Love is holding hands while
Strolling through the meadows of life!
Love is sharing the innermost deepest of secrets
Of two childhoods linked together to became one!
Love is mentally suffering and Caring enough to bare
One another's burdens, together forever!

MR. SUNSHINE

Mr. Sunshine!
You ail me so.
One thousand places I try to hide,
A thousand and one you go.

Don't drain my strength
And bead my brow,
Mr. Sunshine,
Tell me now.

I know that one day
You shall leave
So, to you, for now
I will cleave.

But comes the time
For you to burst
Molten rain upon the earth
As men do think them in their prime.

If you see me scramble
For a little shade
A tree, house, or shelter made
I am not afraid

So, let me
Rest!
Mr. Sunshine,
Sometimes.

DOWN WITH KACEY

Too late for mercies helping hand
Knowledge in your scheming legal plans
Your bed is deep in the under watered well
Where pillows are of cold-hot stone
And forever rotten bodies you may smell

Down with Kacey
I heard the public cry
You had your satisfactions
Now it's your turn to die
Down with Kacey, Down with Kacey
The monster of so many a mothers' eye

I saw more people yelping than
The swell for not believing the sketchers' plan
Your head and heart are weighed
With all their souls you tell
Their milestones hang about your neck
But deserve to be the steppingstone
Of the waterless well

Down with Kacey
I heard the public cry
You had your satisfactions
Now it's your turn to die
Down with Kacey, Down with Kacey
The monster of so many uh mothers' eye

Your face was aired across the lands
You disgraced all good thriving Americans
Folly plants the soul in a furnace lake
The entire world was waiting
Just to hear the final breath you'd take

Down with Kacey
I heard the public cry
You had your satisfactions
Now it's your turn to die
Down with Kacey, Down with Kacey
The monster of so many a mothers' eye

Aren't no pictures cute enough
You could call the whole world's lawyers
But cannot call its' bluff
You lived your life crude and tough
Now that it's your turn to die
You don't look so tough.

CLEARING FIELDS BY NAILS

Coming by thoughts that dispel me
Sawing on the fell tree
Rooted it must be destroyed
It longs to grow though counted void
To react is to remain healthy

All those branches of the base
Was spreading wild all over all the place
(But fruits good did bear)
WAS of the same Eve did share
That not of good nor grace

Trace, roots need sawed asunder
Clipped from base which fed my blunders
Thunders in my chest Crying for some rest
That brought me up to 'fess wonders

Ah yes, the tree has fallen
Whose roots cry in calling,
Calling for some dirt of survival
Uprooted well in deprival
Is dying, Oh, the weight once hauling'

The field now being closed and wheedles
With what good fruit can prevail
By my Saviors Blood I cannot fail
For the actual clearing was,
My name carved in his hand
By Nail!

ALPINE INNER SPIRITS

You were talking alpine in your spirits
While to climate of your cranny heart
Short wired the coils inside your head
Among your peers only, you patronize the dead.

Merely maybe to gain a little merit?
For your apples carried, nobody here will miss
Looks like your climate caused misfiring
First! How heavy is the weight you are aspiring?

So, you say your wit came by osmosis?
Seems to me you're in self-hypnosis
May I suggest a shot of 'un-abyss your heart'
Before you boldly patronize life and death apart

Your apples of knowledge worm down to less than crumb
Alpine is dynamite, volcano Atom bomb
Should you Baskin Robin dip, deep beyond abyss
Unrealistic beyond your bliss
Let's amplify the bolus, to obtain your sum.

12/20/1995

CAUGHT IN A TREND

Years have taken our precious lives
When future reality affects our strives
Past but sees us on our way
Warning: Stray not in a tingle
Was relentless a chol-thought to angle.
Was late to discover, life could have paid…

The tongue outlined this destination
Youth thought to define by illogical inflation
Fought through the fractions of barrier gaps
But the choice of the wild is never straight
Booze before dinner and chow must wait
The mind of all thought retrieves his fate (perhaps).

Death of former, took you to be with we
One step covers years, yet you took in glee
(Should lines been different, then seed in toil)
Light shines in words of your heart
With now reflecting, there is enough time to start
(Perhaps affections could have been more royal)

Overtaken by years, all left in age
Still caught in the trend of the worldly safe
All said and done, with one thing to tell
You gave it your best, I did not so well
Respecting the strength that pulled me through
It has been hell. I am me, and you are you!

JOKER IN THE DEAL

I'm tired and I can't sleep
So sad that I can't weep
Tear ducts have not damp to seep
Into thoughts of my mind
For moments worth of time
Keep the try I find
Below the big blue deep

Alay, awake at night
Alone in thoughts
Chasing memories of life
All these years for nothing right
Chasing memories of my thought
For all that I have sought
To have found sadness so near
No way around it to steer

Look around my new home
It's not all alone
One in a world of drones
Another gear on the brazen wheel
Another shoe on a heel
The lost joker in the deal
This is pestilence, like in the seal

Verily I merely exist
A number on a world of list
But slamming home as a fiat
The tides of my past
Lord knows just how long I can last
Try to change, try to fast
But this old flesh is just so real

Well work my senses to feel
There's a joker in the deal
Doctor… like the one in the seal
Ferocious whirlpool
Intellect sometimes isn't cool
I've been acting like a fool
Over the red no-nourish peel.

BROKEN ON A STICK

It was vague a night of emotion
Running deep in the heart of man
Living by a street devotion
Looking without a plan

He ran up against a fighter
Silly boy, knew bodies were not bullet proof
Like broken on a stick in frigid winter
Mister, he did meet the truth

Happiness! They say, I should write about
Times like this is all I know
Billy led a life of fears, no doubt
From broken on a stick type of home

There are no joyful reminders
Taking him back home in glee
Like broken on a stick, ended Billy's life
That Chicano had no ear for his plea

Ripples on a pond, unnoticed
Until crossing the Mob
And happy was his hostess
Chilly frost' now kiss his blood

You got to read the writing on the wall
He couldn't see a porch for the fog
Now a' ride the sky: a bullet for his sled
Vogue a night of emotional display

FROGGY AND THE ORIOLE

Froggy went down to Blue Lake
Took him a bottle of wine
When he got sown to Blue Lake
Froggy drank him-blue-self blind

Sitting on the sandy shore
Feeling like he was going to die
When leaping lizard came along
And caught to the butterfly

"Oh, pretty winged maiden
Show me the secrets your heart hides
You used to crawl through the gardens
And now you freely float in the skies

Please make me to have some wings
Show me the secrets to make cocoons
So, I can fly to unite my soul
With my truest love, the oriole

Leaping said, "Hey what's happening
For what reason do you cry
Well at least the lake isn't polluted
Yeah! You have to look at the brightest side".

Then the evening dimmed a purple shine
As a tear swelled Froggy's eye
Feeling soon his heart would break
He stayed riveted to his wine

Froggy looked at his walnut shell watch
But time never gave him a clue
"I'm going to sit right here, while my oriole dear
Sings me to death with her blues…

Cause he knew she was a flyer
While his life was lake and limbs
But he got so tired of only sitting beside her
Just to watch her sail away again.

LETTER TO A FRIEND

The mailman called out loud and lean
"Mail call!", then proceeded calling names
Busy was I, in a cooling sprawl
Reading (study), Searching deep within aim
It was not mother, brother, nor Pa.
But it came!
My book? I laid not on its face,
But cared to mark the page;
Up a-top my book in dread,
Then took your letter from my bed.

To my surprise before my eyes
I held a story all untold
And commenced to take in the pictures…
While the pictures did unfold.
I saw somebody singing softly To a melody so fair.
When the tune touched my ears
My heart went to humming thunderously;
It was you behind those ivory keys.
As your own music you did mold!

Many tales once told, would sooth the soul
But few would make the mind,
Like, "The convict came back after the fall".
Who can find the will to remain?
The same; But the man with aim!
So, the bamboo flute breaths golden sound
Like no whistle ever found
And the acoustic guitar, by way and far
Can still make the amplifier frown.
"Those untouched tunes in your head? jot them down!"

To see myself on those pages, plain and raw
(Sometimes I cannot imagine how)
But I can decipher that I saw Sounds appear as words.
And know for what or how
(Other than the calming of disturbed)
You are truly the artist
As I reach deep beneath my pen
Still the amateur
To bring out what's inside

Health is up and down a water slide
If, the devils are inhaled
The mount of another man's pride.
In this I set to lay them down.
Ran laps until my heart thought burst
And ran my way up quite high.
Now I cough and choke and hurt
Through many a sleepless night
To the point where neighbors don't sleep.
I'm left to wonder what is right.

First, I know that I come first
"No! That's Jesus Christ"
And the man beside me
Prays daily on his knees
But those stabbing remarks aren't nice.
So, turn to little whines Stories like these.
God only knows, where goes what gifts
He has ready to provide.
To keep what sane
The little I've left, on prayers roll my tide.

To teach is to master, be it work or art
And everyone who master
 Must contribute their part.
To teach is to excel the standard
Set by all who work and play
Forming the mind, does seldom find
One to take it all the way
To teach is to master
Master creating what you like to play
And play to please heaven every day!

Three-thirty-three (am) signing off once more
Throat is smoke raw, my mind is sore
I've coughed so much my gut is a knot
My lungs are in unloving war.
Take care! To yourself be true
You're the best human friend you've got
To be untrue to ourselves, we have no lot
So, spend some time with yourself.
Have you your best friend fought?
Learn what you feel, from ado.
In Christ, Love Allot!

THE HUBCAP MAN

When the hubcap man no more
Sets of the painting of your car
Remember the days when chrome displayed
Much of who you are
But in the modern grind of new space time
Many things must fall

Many things must fall before
The modern trend of time.
The mag wheels knocked out the hubcap
And cost more than a dime
But where is all our proudness when chloride clouds
Burn your breathing air
Guess the hubcap man went out with fender flairs.

Down the road a country mile or so:
All faded and worn,
Is a broken shock with graves out back!
Where cars' cars were second
But the hubcap man is pushed from the land
By aluminum, all onyx
Where is the hubcap man today to help your boys?

Now days, stage coaches and cowboys
No longer sets the theme.
The statutes of war are no more
A nightmare but a dream.
The wheel still turns, as bullets burn
Through the heart of change
When the hubcap man no longer gets a ring.

Many things must fall before
The tread of modern time
Computers are more amazing than
Any windblown chime
When there's a brick, in your microchip
How are you going to steer?
When the new wears off, your shiny alloy wheels?

SALAD OF DREAMS

Life isn't all it seems
Salad of living dreams
Spider web of I-beam steel
I resume to reveal

Pallid thoughts contain
Things that shine or stain
I fain to quote it
All they must conceal

Lifeline to what esteems
House of hollow things
Splendor web of I-beam steel
Entwined to a seal

Mallet of exquisite
Driving against the mark
Inner web stand stark
Strong against ordeal

Dream is a founder
By earnest of the eye
That's an astounder
Meditation confounder

Look fell on the dream
First thing the eye esteemed
Was the salad of dreams!
There a part will all

They're not dead when green
Energy from something else
Averaging in health
Or living on the brown shelf.
Salad of dream so pallid
Molded against the valid
Folded the eye of solid
Image of the dream.
Dream is to reveal
To eye where to steer
Eye then marks it down
Earnestly make it sound

So, that lark in the dark
Isn't such a shark
To what really reveals
And the eye resumes to conceal.

An eye made the horizon
One that dare to dream
Didn't put no lies in
Looking glass of dream.

Bread all horizons
I fain to quote
It's not blind to note
Dreaming is an antidote.

All they conceal
I resume to reveal
Splendor web of I-beam
Spider web of the dream.

IRON BRICK

Hmm! You saw the look I gave
I want to be your sucker, slave?
To patrol your pretty cave
As you give me a shove,
And a shake and a shift
So much you make me uplift
Let you be my gift
I will be your craze.

Babe it's what-not like it seems
I want to tell you all my dreams
Just don't ask what it all means
Cause I don't know baby
When I saw you in your seams!
My eyes contacted dream
I thought to touch by any means
Um, but then they say I'm crazy

Crazy for that look you deal
Crazy for just how I feel
I just want to reveal
What I felt when you went by
Was a heal of a deal
Think I saw what I hope you feel
To one another we appeal

Now this may sound sort of numb
But out there you're just a crumb
To be picked off by some dumb…
Cause they have no taste of love
But I will love you till you're numb
Let me be your tables crumb
Your big crazy, dangerous bum
Someone like you baby, I long to love

It's all around you if you look
Another story in a never-ending book
Don't get snared on their hook
I know you are thinking, "What's the trick".
I just can't forget your look
"That guys' a story book".
So, what is new, can we make it work.
Only for you I am an Iron Brick.

CONTRAST EMPTINESS

The night was silent and pleasant
An air of most comfort to breath
A season of summer filled peasants
Deserts full of sage (tumble weeds)
Together we sought in negligence
A heart to wit with which to play
Uncaring for the outcome of undue season
We reasoned with emotions display

The sky revealed sight of the heavens
Stars and the moon on display
This night, on my heart could lay no graver
Yet must I carry on this way
Lights from uncounted days of glimmer
The trees motioned us on our way
Therefore, we spring forth without stammer
Springing forth to play

Needing no kind of conversation
Concentration on the beauty arrayed
Our hearts beating passionately
So clearly, I see you this way
Anxious and willing for giving
Our breath on the windows
Grew thicker than clay
To still hear them, your whispers…
"Shouldn't Have left you, I know
Now, that I have gone away".

I realize now, how much I love you
Reminiscing of our lives we shared
I stare to the sky, clouds glistening
And mourned in my heart of despairs
As the sun marches on silent
Thus, I am in this loneliness
This, contrast emptiness.

SEE NO ALL

Hear no nothing
See no all
Fear no human will
Know wanting
Summer and fall

Tell no whoppers
Talk through the walls
Little bug on the windowsill
Hear my thoughts
Would you ever answer?
It would really chip my cogs

Hear no nothing
See no all
Feel no want
No willingness to break the law

Watching flipper
From down the hall
Little frogs on my front lawn
I'm listening
Would you answer to a word?
It would really chip my cogs

I hear no nothing
See no all
Feel of will
Know haunting, for breaking laws

I know haunting
And it really chips my cogs
I know I couldn't rightly say
But think I was
Haunted by the frogs
And it really chips my cogs

OPUS

Color an opus of blooming wealth
Fresher than breath to a newborn baby
Fill it with crisis and mystery
Touch it with the magic of love for all
Save your inert and obtuse feathers

Not one word therein to move my heart
A thunderous tune, clear, blue, breezy
Reduce no supreme note of beauty
With earths evil, dark, morose deeds
Of man's hearts (For cherubs do play harps)

Color an opus in flight, soft and free
Choose to express to myself how I feel
Keep your stones that weight souls in abyss
Fill it, your heart there lie, however:
Keep free to sore with an opus.

MOONBEAM LOVE

So, like moonbeams in rays of the sun,
Unseen like my true love, my only one:
Have I searched for, omni scopic and wide!
Like the moonbeam shines forever at my side.

I once found a beam; she burned so bright in my heart,
That coals of bitterness had molten to swart.
She did outshine the brightest of bright.
Set my state in such a glee, I did up and plight:

To leave that fair land, if I could not win her heart.
Approached her in every angle, more cunning than art.
Pleading on account, of loves powerful force.
Guided by such a strong thing I had no choice.

I left there that fountain that could spring me to life.
Left there a doubting, I'd ever have a wife.
Up jumped the junky, which gave no wares.
Searching for true love, coming up with tares.

Then plucked out weeds arose in my passions.
Departure of each growth took a piece of fashion.
Though my love has been beaten up and torn:
I'll search for my moonbeam, till I'm withered and worn.

© February 21-1993

SNAFU

Too many tom-toms in the tower, cried the maid
as she tumbled in the air
But her opponent wasn't weary for
 Single thing she said.
Her nose was powdered, paint covered
The black around her eyes
Another trembling handmade it's way
Up along her thighs.

He never noticed when she winced
Nor heard her soul begin to wail
Her body moved as gentle waters
Over stones, her Trojan fears inside
Disguised themselves as moans
His only care was having a whore of his own
All she knew was, she had to feed
Five mouths at home
All he felt was the pleasure, in the body
He used.
All she knew was great relief when
Money crossed her palm.

Nobody knows why, we do the things we do
Man is so quick to point the finger of fault
We never see behind the scene
Only the players upon the stage
So long as there's a curtain
We can see whatever we want

As she cleaned and dressed herself
He mumbled: "Freaking whore".
His trousers dragged across his knees
She whispered: "God forgive him please?"
And me once more

And once again: "Good bitch"
As she closed the door
All the same her heart was crying
He doesn't even know my reason Lord
Why I must work the floor

RELIGION

Paint me up the world of faces
Title me ten thousand times
Leave me in empty buildings' disgraces
Exploit me in your rhythm and rhymes

Carry me before all your critiques
Dress me in a world of wallet green
But do not take me out to your operas
Cause I'm not the center of your scene

Call me coined by all seven countries
Shun how nations change my name
Faire in their wars called righteous
Now isn't that a claim?

Peace doesn't kill, or haven't you heard?
It is the essence of all hearts being still
The essence of the spoken word
Don't color me to the seeds of your will

Where I pit the rich and flog the poor
Converted to the cause of racist
Make me a caterer to the house of the whore
Paint me up an entire world of faces

I introduced man to a higher living
And you would wear me down to the earth
But beware of your subtle misgiving
Lest I become not your faith, but your curse.

3/22/1995

NIGHT STOLE MY FACE

When mine can't even walk
It ran my name to the ground
All its sounds echo in the rocks
Some names mean everything-mine can't talk

They can fling their flares over all pages
Mine goes scarred to no repair
No certitude' can change that dude
While I'm the only one to care

Stare into the darkest night
That's all I'm worth to look at me
Se the trees, and summers to please
Everyone there survives of his might

When mine cannot even talk
That it has been ran into the ground
Must it be changed to Lie, or Socrates?
And use that till reaching my churchyard park

Staring into the dark
At the heart of wrong for so long
It's always attaching me
But it is dead to the Arts

Most can fling their faces over pages
But night as stole my face
By a hair of the dog that bit me
Left me in corner some place

Yet the dark of night was my teacher
That features all we embark
In the Arts, there's a measure of grace
I steal from the night who stole my face.

WE DO NOT SEE

What is the cost? What is the cause?
How much to wager, how high the odds?
And looking always, we do not see,
Someone there back staring me.
Wonder who just might become
Wranglers with seals on their thumb?
Just use a number, nothing will change.
Would you still call him so free?

Where are the watchmen, where are my wings?
What says the bluebird whenever he sings?
And looking don't always we see;
Something that always will be?
Some part of history will somehow up and come,
Giving out one more of life's ways to blame.
Just look around, see where to aim…
But then would you still call them free?

We shared the past, I bore the pain
Now left to swim through my eyes of rain.
When looking there always I feel,
An orange is no orange, till away with its peel.
Now I know there can't come nothing new
What is the cost, what is the cause?
Who wants to wager, how many will crawl?
Back to her beauty, while your freedom she steals?

And looking always we don't see
Someone there back staring me.
The picture is painted, the canvas is dry
The figure is immobile, but don't blink an eye
On to her beauty you crawl as she steals.
Just use a number, who expects a seal?
How much to wager what it reveals?
And looking always we don't see!

UNCLE PAUL

I have dreamed but all my life
Now decided to pursue
That old dream is a knife
Chopping my sanity in two

After watching your high talent play
Jamming to the songs of your youth
Came a time, I had told myself
I'm gonna be like you

The songs on the beat box buzz my mind
Full of rhythms and blues
Been calling on me with all I wrote
A couple even ran around in my shoes

So, a cheap guitar, all but garbage to none
Found its way to my fingers review
They stumbled and stepped around stairwells of sound,
Stammered then stepped to the blues

My step was broken by a tower of time
My soul chokes unable to chime
After dreaming all my life
I deem necessary to pursue

SPRYLING

What have you Spryling, but youth?
That two-tone age after boyhood
When we learn of life and truth
More a child as we step into manhood

It is only given one time
For man to pass through pupilage
Into adolescence there find
One day to playing the next out of working

A shooting star I have beheld
Wishing there, come true my dreams
For a span suddenly felt
There is more to life than seems

There are so many children unprepared
Compared to some so finely tuned
Whom but blindly stagger down the stair
To an unwholesome city of ruin

Catch a falling star and put it in your pocket
So, all the world has heard
Do not mock it
They are a precious group of words

Our newness must someday turn antique
As the pages of a new book smell unturned
As it is used, its vigor grows weak
Its leaf's anxiety already learned

What have you Spryling but youth…?
Cherish it! Rainy days must come
Live to learn while you are young
In addition, in age you will be strong.

FORTY FEET BABY

Take a walk, forty feet out the driveway honey
Before you come to bitch at me
I have Always known what you're searching for?
But argument does not stimulate me

Just walk forty feet from the garage door
To that warning weeping willow tree
You know what his name is carved there for,
Since the year Nineteen- Eighty-Three

Our marriage has lasted on my strength alone
Ever since you chained my finger down
What you wanted was a working yuppie
What you have is a weeping willow tree

Ten years yesterday, since I found you at play
When you threw out the key to our love
Just walk forty feet baby, down the way
To remember what I keep thinking of

If forty feet is too much to ask for
Then my stepping stipulation becomes reality
Only forty feet from the garage door, baby
Before you come to bitch at me

You can read it aloud if you like
But don't ever read it to me
Should it ever happen that I go to stepping
Just go read his name on your tree

1994

PRISON BULLY

Cradled in your misery
Fighting down your pain
Your armor is the hurt you bring
On the man who can do what you cannot

You cannot humble yourself
Prides and fears get in your way
You put your heart on your shelf
When you fell that day, away.

I've seen your type before
So bad by the tongue, yet insecure,
Will pick at another in unawares
Enticing the devil's lure

Impress your friends; what a mode!
Being wise in your own choice
When picking roads
To exercise your voice

Selected to go down
Bullyism, you walked in
Bullyism, you found.
Remember the code

Do error not, to gender this way
Within the thought
"With lives I play"
Lest I breath your air of tomorrow today.

1992

THE END

Acid rain fell in those times
Melted gold was found by the score
It was Russia not Iraq
Men were few and woman fewer
Demons roamed the earth with power
Over man to hurt, and not kill
Destruct and not destroy, at will.
The trees and grass were unharmed.
Mother earth cried for relief
Of the burden she bears of Man-Kind.
Skin burned but did not decay
The dead and the living walked the earth
Together, seekers of useless gold
Obsessed by their passion of greed
Their lust money knew not
That soon their souls would burn
They searched in great desire
They found forevermore
The mineral so loved and killed for.
I told the preachers
But they could not hear, and smirked me off
In disbelief that I could know that
The time is near. While people
So many, were strong in their ways
But I have shelter, Shelter from the storms.
I have shelter in the blood of Jesus
On the cross of Christ.
I walk through these times unharmed.

©1992 (This piece was an actual dream which I had some time in 1992)

SOCIETY

Society, says I
As my heart drips dry
Clutches deafly to my life
Choking out my goals
Tugging on my soul
And I'm in no position to fight.

Still fight yet I must
Goes all win or bust
Too long have I played their game!
And played by my rules
Cause I was the fool.
Now I'm out to take back my name!

1983

NEGATIVITY

O'er the darkness of a moonlit night
Engulfing hearts the more
Blinding aspects of light deplore
Questions knowledge, to what delight

Essence of battles valor
Navigates about rooms, drone to drone
Refusing there to advance
Feeding doubt of all that is known
By skepticisms, life be lanced
Unconsecrated, un-grown.

(Oh! Go breath denial! Prerequisite
To such attitudes, till death incline
hat defying allures the pit.)
Erase the progression, per the blind,
Negativity is, but the sum of it!

August 17-1992

SIGNATURES

Address your signature on one side of the page
The top is eternal life
If you rightly can sign either half
Then can your *autograph* be saved

Palms together, the top hand
Touches the ink you saved
The left will fell, horror your reveal
From the bonds that have you enslaved

Address your signature on the page
The hand in red ink on the right
The darkness of black, the left
But the cleft of my chest, cannot divide the two
I just have not, that kind of might!

MASTER O' FLAWS

There's a cracker with a crunch
You should follow your hunch
Before you tackle him
Bring your breakfast and lunch

Driftwood with a cause
Allow me to pause
When you're speaking to him
Speak to the master of flaw

Driftwood on the seas
Of human trees
Whose roots all return
To the unlearned seas

A cause put to jaw
He adheres to no law
Just can't define this
Time has not missed, master of flaw

There's a cracker with a hunch
All the world could be crunched
Who would sit around!
Sipping whiskey and punch

All "could be" craze for a cause
Contrast of the laws
All so far to be found
Just a master of flaw

A master of flaw
Legend to none
From minus zero
To negative one

Just a master of flaw
An empty hero
Don't be thorns in the paw
Your credit card's ghetto.

SACRED DREAM

Mamma please don't go
To the place were
I should have gone
You're the best
Fiend I've ever had

I will not be late
And just can't live
With the thought
Hold my hand
Till I reach the Promised Land

Are you sure?
That you are ready
or the peaceful shore?
I was told to question
Are you in the light?

I cried last night
Tears as free as flow, for you
Please, where father went
Please don't go

Please don't go
To that awful place
Where all should have gone
You're the best
Friend I've ever had.

WHEN FUTURE COMES

The sounds of freedom make their image
Un-auditory enough to hear.
Engines, running water, shouts, murmurs,
Barking of some distant dog,
Laughing, the squeaking sign moving
Robust in a howling wind…
After some amount of time.
I roam the land, run, dance and sing with all.
Moving along the mull of the crowd.

The mounds of workmanship spring forth
Forming dozens of castles in the grass
The earth turned inside out
From the pillowed dungeon.
The grisly sun makes his presence known
Ornamenting forever…
The Constantine sparkles of life, momentarily
A clear blue sky brings the scene of peacefulness.
While a blue grayish haze waits over the horizon.
Transcending into the perfect blue above…
The forest is quiet.

Voices echo from the past.
Players roar out from the game.
Shouts and scream bring me back.
The sun travels unnoticed overhead.
The rush of running water clapping its hand
For the sun's departure unaccounted
Runs off to leave us.
Leaves us once again, as has the world,
Just as I am here,
With a world existing only in my head
The same as this present will survive
When… future comes.

DUCK, DUCK GOOSE

Duck, Duck Goose
A willow and a spruce
Side by side together in a field
Together came some feathers
Looking for a roof
A truthful place to rest their heels.

They could not use clever
But which one do they choose?
Or do you think it any big deal
Living on the limb
A little in the weather
Never a moment to steel

Living life in letters
Can't ever leave my youth
Doing the dance of, rest my heels
It never gets any better
Doing my best to dodge harsh weather
And scrape up another meal

Duck, Duck, Duck Goose
A trigger and a truce
A combination I had hoped to feel
Together with a hammer
Took away to muse
One more spin on the great big wheel.

ATTIRE ASPIRED

Contact! Came your eyes
Briefly and pleasantly plain
You showed there your sacred skies
You need somebody to rein
And I felt, "Conspire"
Swelling from deep down inside
I can't extinguish the fire
Cause I have no tears left to rain.

Drug out go the nights
Until I have you
To show you a sacred right.
The things I think I go through
To what I aspire
Cling to you with all my might
Only for you am I for hire
And I promise all of this is true

Know what hell it is
New year will never change
You showed me your side, now consider this
Are you aware of the range?
Of your young attire
New year will surely drain?
When you're no longer desired
Too late, your already strange.

Girl, I can see you tomorrow
Without my losing constraint
Already on a line too narrow
Slowly losing my point
And I think to use the arrow
It's obvious, I'm no saint
But down to my marrow, I am the fool
Conspiring to taint our pool.

STATUE OF WAR

Dust has changed the road sign
Words only half appear
Follow that man with the white cane
Who is going nowhere!
I wondered what he had thought on,
To be stranded that way
Unable to discern
Midnight forms into day

If the voice inside is crying
Why doesn't anyone care?
Will the voice inside keep trying?
To help you get there from here.
Too much dust on the yellow brick road
For me to follow the sign.
Does it really show, where the highway goes?
That he will never find?

Does he see a still voice cry?
Does he hear the sign pointing the way?
Only a replica of what once was
Another statue of the day.

I saw him standing in the street
Icy rain had taken his face.
Frigid and shaking, he stands concrete
As he went no place.
Wonder why that voice don't call him,
Given a sword to fight the bomb
Walking in vogue, on a dirt brick road
Where yellow has faded to bronze.

Statue of war, what do you stand for?
Just a replica that seems
Knowing more than any, what is sure?
The sign of death to too many of young man's dreams.

NATURES STATEMENT

Is that a statement?
Or, am I at flaw?
Beyond abasement
Don't break the law.

Do YOU make neurosis?
Or keep me "in" sane?
You are a hypnosis,
This is clearly plain.

Whose eyes see it all?
Your silent gestures
Are your natural calls
That are statements to a higher law.

It has taken some moments
To fully understand
Your natural intents.
Even dark exist not, without light on the stand.

Her hand is extended
For you to grab
Do not be offended
If at first it feels drab

When nature makes a statement
Actions are correct
And when they are profound,
The more nature subjects to her crown.

Is that a statement?
Or, am I at flaw?
Great heights in abasement
Nature offers us all.

BROWN SCARS

The bear roared out in protest.
Wise old owl just sat and watched.
The wolf went to howling, how he'd had enough,
"Don't cut any more forest
'Oh Man', You ruin everything you touch".

When then they'd settled all their clowning.
Owl floated down from his perch,
Quoting what he had caught wind of
While he in town watching ways of earth.
Then began he, praising, Plumb Creeks efforts!

Bear retorted in quibble and grumble
Owl acquired silence *with a feather.*
Wolf shouted," Why should I care for forest,
It'll be gone before me? Then in a mumble,
"See you know not one human thing".

"They will leave some trees", said Owl, "of some species.
But we must let man pass the test.
If there ever will be, new forestry's,
Then their brown scars can heal and rest.
Although man must first pass our test.

The forest is turning over a new leaf.
The hobbits of wildlife preserved.
Old forest in new forestry,
Awakening from its sleep.
Gone around the mill yet growing the hill wisely conserved.

UNFAITHFUL FATHER

How could you have set this in my heart?
As I worked until my brow was wet,
You were at my home abusing me.
How could you still look into my eyes?

While we sat, there on the riverbank
Waiting on the fish to bite
Were you laughing to yourself?
Knowing you knew the joy of my life.

How could you face your grandson?
Did you tell his grandma you were out for pool?
Or maybe, hanging out with the boys:
Or did you tell her you have been so coy?

I should have known by the beam in your eye
My chariot you were looking to ride
I should have known by your propositions so light;
That my own male parent was jealous of my wife!

TO REMEMBER

When I went to shake your hand
The grey goose had made her show.
Once more I stand, alone.
Looking into more minds, I remember
A lonely boy plying on the snow.
Man, how it used to frighten me,
My little mind did churn,
Every time dad did hit the road;
Knowing that that one loyal friend
May never be found again…
Is it kind of funny though?
How life fills the beaten-up heart
With the heaviest load.
Thirty years and my brothers' still my friend
Two weeks, and my friend becomes a brother.
What does it all mean?
On with intermission
On our way to wait
As before, I knew you would vanish
While terrible tales coursed our veins
Toppling over the tongue.
My mind's eye researched,
To find the past as present.
You asked. I quote
"For something to remember myself by".
Sitting on the wallet
That something now makes me…
Think, how two can be brothers
In less than a day
As two can be brothers for years
And still be friends.
What does it all mean?
Liked the stones we kicked
We have no certain landing

An un-destined stay.
Frightened no more of the unknown
My mind still churns
In return still waiting.
And when I went to shake your hand
Grey goose made her show
So! Here is something to remember me by.

REALITY RHYMES

As all hate is red
All the world is yellow
Afraid of a trend
They kill their man fellow

Jack and Jill
Bought the pill
Purchased for a dollar
To kill their seed
Then feel the need
To sit at the clinics and holler

Little Miss Muffat
Using her tuffet
To get a piece of the pie
She is too lazy to rough it
So, she fakes a tear in her eye

He's a little ditty
Some cat played the fiddle
But to talk out he had no room
So, he wrote up a riddle
And there in the middle
Said his babe ran away with some goon

Jack is nimble
He's so quick
To con the public
He will tread and trick

Hickory dickory Doc
The boat delivered the rock
Till the rat came around
And bring another heavy down
Now time has fell from the clock

HARLOT OF THE ARTS

SH! The harlot of the arts will play now.
At strokes of genius fans all dance
Lashing out at peace, love and romance
In one symbolic slamming dance
Until their bones find dirt to lay.
They're paid a lifetime in advance
Half the world in bonded trance
As the harlot hates the light of day.

By your hatchet strings, you split the heart
With mental monopoly games
Hiroshima - haven earth
You tell it there in your names
You vocalize what you think it's worth
Searching the mysterious for some fame
Never a time to think of birth
While you sign it all off in blood and flame.

The harlot of the arts will play now
Searching for a string
Their metaphors of liaison
Souls are tied to your ball and chain
The lion's young all fill your den
Understanding nothing that you say
However, will run along in liaison
While the devil tricks you, you play.

BROKEN GUITAR

I cannot describe it
I'm turning inside out
My heart was full of sulfur
I can't extinguish the bout.

I knew I shouldn't do it
Intuition said it was wrong
While the anger of my spirit
Kept coming on strong

Anger stomped my guitar
I put my haven in the ground
Peace of soul its music gave me
Ever far on its wave

I cannot describe it
A pleasure in my heart
Cut away now by a fit
And I am yet to fall apart

I knew I shouldn't do it
All intuition said it wrong
But the anger of my spirit
Kept coming on strong

Reflexes took to whiskey
Staggered through the night
All because of jealousy
Stories from my guitar will never see the light.

IN ALL YOUR WAYS

Hold your head high
Walk with dignity son
Hate your neighbor for the shade of his skin
Don't tell any lies
Oh, what a way to begin

Fight the govern-intent
Never steal boy
Take all you can get when it's free
Oh, your mothers a bitch
Honor your parents
What kind of psycho have you made of me?

Fight for respect
Turn the other cheek
They should have fired him last week
Don't love for money
Don't' grow lazy
Why couldn't I have been born rich?

Stay away from drugs Boy bring me a beer
Take some Aspirin, it'll be all right
Respect the law
I couldn't believe we were busted
Let's go watch the movies, see them kill all night

Smoking is bad for you
Never say I'm sorry
The dog is always man's best friend
Trust nobody boy
You always need someone to depend on
What a way to begin!

Educate yourself
How do you spell "it"?
Learn about history
Who shot Jesse James?
Who shot Kennedy?
What kind of psycho would you make of me?
"Take a good look around
Before they grow up, they are knocked down
In all your ways
You contradict everything you say
What we are teaching our children
Is why they are crazy today!

In all your ways.
In all your ways you say conform
Go to church and reform
But in all your ways you illustrate
Lie and steal. Lust and cheat
Greed and pride and hate

In all your ways you say reform
But to your words you don't conform
In all your ways
All your ways
Your ways
Ways

Live for today
When tomorrow comes
All the kings' heroes and honest men
Yesterday's gone
Learn from the past
It'll never be broken again.
© 1-29-1995

I'M ONLY ME

You may see me in a crowd
Just another passer by
Listen to hear my talk aloud
But stop, to think
Within the blink of
You never see my eyes

It's best to not consider me
The same as all the rest
No hair, the same, without a style
A custody code, blue shirt dress
Your figurative one-track mind
Seeing not the mind, but the vest

Just because I'm in the hot water
Does not mean that I too am wet.
If I smile, you call me happy
While frowns portray the next
If I walk with Kings or prisoners
Does not mean I am like the rest.

6-3-1995

CHANGER

This, a drunkard's restless world
You may think it kind of strange
But it is my only reality
So quickly I can change

At once from being kind,
As jolly as a child
Then lose my remembering mind
To turn to as uncaring wild

Why does it have to rule me?
I cannot honestly say
Every bottle seems to fool me
To make me believe, one more will be OK.

UNDERWENT TRUST

I KNOW! I DO NOT TRUST!
Why? Why should I make fuss?
A bro, there to commit sin
No air to intake.
Wet vice did this back break?
Spring up in the so old dark
Pound, pound, pounding went my heart.
Foul water, like earths dirt
One, two times, then three.
UP, PUSH, there, I reach, breath
I cannot, like this stop. STOP!
Touching toes well below top
No air there to breathe. Wait!
Slowly a stones weight
Sore spirit, the mind rent
DOWN, DOWN, DOWN I went!

© 1-9-1995

PICK MASTER

Come and hear a song everybody!
"Say what does it tell?"
The history of the picker man.
And it says it very well

Come and hear the story boys:
One told without using words.
But you can feel when something happens
When he is digging at some chords

Settle down to hear a master
Plucking at his heart strings
A master doesn't have to speak
Because his guitar sings…

CHRISTIAN READING

Found in the daily papers
Is death from hate and greed?
Lust and gluttony fill the streets
Each day for lost souls to read

Seen on the big screen it is the same
Garbage, fights, games; no operas:
Filling hearts with damnations
Must have been the likeness when the great flood came

Novels of passions' fashions, lies
Even books for old babies,
But there is only one book we're needing
"The Bible",

Gives our best Christian Reading.

MATURE DEW

Look at me! Look at you!
The Atlantic once was the dew.
But back to the heavens God had it sent
For His precious blades of grass were bent
Loaned for a time like me and you
And if we do not bring life, we die
It is our only chance to sail the sky

So! When you see me falter?
Or if you see me fail
Please do not come, just to scold
I am keenly aware
I know the fool I am
Doesn't please the Lord
So, pray for me to grow.
Lord, help me to mature?

AN INFORMAL SENTIENT

An informal sentient
That don't mean he is blind
Got a million dependents
Their always on his mind.
Always a story to invent
In whatever he finds
Using what intents, you have
Your fairest emotions, these are his salve

The informal sentient
He is one of our own
Only thing of resentment
Is being so alone
Each day, the same advent
A woman's love he's never known
For all of life he does care
His whole life is emotion, seen from a chair

Wasn't no accident
Just dealt his hand of fate
Never made one crying statement
He was born that way.
The in formal sentient
Watch the animals play
Saying "At least I have a mind.
And with it all the glorious things I find".

Your heart will circumvent
To his subtle grace
Don't allow his legs of cement
To get in the way
A real social sentient
Meeting the daily grind.
If only the world were so kind.
With it the glorious things we could find.

RAILS TO GLORIOUS

Jonah in the belly of the whale
Daniel in the lion's den
Jesus Christ did pay my bail
Lord, I know you're coming again!

God never lies I know for sure
Jesus never faltered once
God is the Father of peace and love
We must give him every ounce

Moses in the far wilderness
Joseph in the prison deep
Gods Son has given us new life
For all the world He weeps

Hebrew children in the fiery furnace
Christ upon that rugged cross
Jesus gave all heavens' entrance
I know my soul will never be lost

So, climb on aboard Gods Holy Train
And ride the rails to glorious
One hand on the wheel of faith
The other on the throttle of love.

PAST, PRESENT, FUTURE

Life is a walk through many valleys
What endless mountains one must climb
Such terrible tolls we often tally
That craters of good remain but crumb

An onslaught of terrain before us
Trails of struggles behind
Looking back cannot only detour us
But keep troubles ahead in the blind

Just some, should the eye overtaken
And work so far ahead as to lose
Heart in the very steps we are takin'
Come the hardest falls by the least slip of shoes

Walks of rarity are not from phobias
Keep eyes on our now-steps we compass
Look not behind nor ahead to woe
Let each step be, now rewarding, please so!

MY FLOWER IS HIS LOVE

Texas has its yellow rose
Marriage a corsage
Death's flower contains all of those
With a mirror of mirage.

But I have been redeemed
I am reborn Yes!
I have been saved
My flower is God's love.

The NAVY has its fleets of ships
And an Atom bomb
But war cannot change none of this
It's only greed's mirage.

But I have been changed
I've been received
I am my Fathers adopted son
My armor is his love.

America claims the eagle
But its TV feeds me crow
Though pride still cross my path
Testing God up above

I have been freed
From sin I tug
It is a relief
By the power of Christ's love

I have been freed,
 Changed, Redeemed
By His Innocent Blood
My flower is His Love!

NO SEEMING

There is no seeming "The Lord Jesus"
As what appears so, is real.
Walls have fallen Lord:
But arise in other fields.
I thank you for calling me!
Walking the walk most difficult,
We are constantly at war with the enemy
Within and without.
All around us is your name used in vain,
Hard and empty hearts.
There's no place to reach solitude,
No place to be alone!
In my closet I confide in my Lord,
And all becomes well.
Troubles go away.
The closer I grow to the most Holy Lord,
God heaven and earth,
The more each wrong thing stands out,
Seeming all, to be directed at myself;
Stumbling blocks.
The more which presses a-fold
The more I count, and call on Jesus:
Because there is no seeming,
As what appears is real.
All is directed toward Christ Jesus
Who walked the perfect walk!
He has set me free.
I praise you Lord to walk with me.
I am but an insect,
But your creatures are yours.
Sometimes I become despondent
From my afflictions
I am constantly reminded
Of past deviltries

That I came from a bad seed.
Thank you, Lord, for showing me
And making me not to forget
Unless I should again fall.
Jesus walk with me…

September 6-1992

CRY PRAISES TO THE LORD

Singing birds in feathered apparel
Blue Jay, humming or sparrow
Appealing to my senses shelter,
Finding no place for welter,
Want, or kind of any need.
Songs of joy, chirping free, "I am free".
Just perceive their happiness
Alight upon limbs abreast
The great blue sky
A hand affixed over their lives
To meet their every want
Be it food or cover, need not hunt
They only acquire of vast supply
Reproduce and cry,
Cry praises to the Lord.
This is how I long to be
Although incarcerated, I am free.
When affliction presses fold
I bow my head and grasp ahold
The wings of life that carry me
Through days of stress
Through fields of weeds.
Lifting me up, when my spirit is down
I am given a smile to replace this frown.
Receiving happiness of vast supply
From pain I am loosed, and cry,
Cry praises to the Lord.

WASH MY HEART AT NIGHT

When I wash my heart at night,
Before taking on the bed:
Wringing out the worldly dirt;
That fell from heart and head.

Sometimes, I feel like a solar system
Has been lifted from my shoulders;
As I go drifting,
In the mighty Spirit of God.

Sometimes when I am listening
I hear Him whisper
And I go drifting
In the Mighty Spirit of God.

Then, when I open my eyes at light
Before stepping out of bed
I take the mighty Words of Christ
In thanks for being fed.

It feels like a solar system,
Has been sat upon my heart
However, I still hear His whisper
"This is where you start".

Sometimes, I go through day
Gleaming, glowing and glistening.
Other days, I seem to forget what I have.
What is missing then is, I forget His healing Hand.

And when I wash my heart at night
Before taking on the bed,
I wring out the dirt
That fell from my heart to my head.

BIBLE WISE

I mute to run, through the sun
With the dabbles of my mind
Search and seize, nouns to please.
Not one could I find.

I mute to run through the sun
Of the cradles of my heart:
There, must shun, rely on the Son
Allow me not torn apart.

I delve to books, lot shelves in nooks
There yet no wit to learn.
I trust to taste, the Spice so great
Either live right or burn.

Lo nature and be for sure,
The skies, the sun and the sea
Gain the truth in age and youth
There is only one way to be free.

So, run the pages of most ancient ages
Need you knight or sage.
But there is more wit in our breath
The helping hand of strength and health.

© February 19-1993

TEACH ME LEARNING LORD

Enlighten ME OH Lord my God
Your precious word to study through
Awaken joyously my broken heart
Renew my spirit, crippled blue.

There comes a day in much man's lives;
And some luckily, a time or two,
God's great grace may will find
He will know what God has planned; He sees through.

Excel within against what you despise
Excite in me to contemplate…
Clean this flesh that ails me so
May I to your word learn and relate.

August 30-1992

ROBE OF SNOW

Here am I again

Alive in sin

But that's not the way

I chose to go.

Lord I can't wait

To see pearly gates

And to wear

That robe of snow.

WONDER NO MORE

Wonder, wonder, wonder enough
Then you'll know
Where does He come from?
Where does He go.

Wonder, wonder, wonder search and
Then you'll see
There's no one higher up
Then you and me.

Wonder, wonder, wonder, praise God
Let your light show
The power of Jesus
Holy Spirit flow.

Wonder, wonder, wonder aloud
Let us sing
Our glorious Jesus
Is Lord and King.

Wonder, wonder, wonder no more
In heart nor soul
Christ Jesus the Lord has it
Under control.

Wonder, wonder enough Jesus
Is the way
He will return for His children
And take us away.

Wonder, wonder, wonder no more
I know why he's King
He gave His life for us
To be free.
(April 28-1992)

SIGN OF THE TIMES

Look into the stars
Signs of the times.
Faster, flip the cards
Tell me what is mine?
Astrology tells me I'm blind
But I can see so far.

What's your aspect on Mars?
Does it affect me today?
Do I gain wealth?
Maybe find a love?
If I had power,
Would I push, pride and shove?

A castle above the clouds
To study heavens yard
When is the big space pow-wow?
Taxi shuttle cars.

Fortresses of metal
Beyond the age of stone
Guided by a medium,
Man wants heaven as his own.
But when all is leveled
You cannot hide in the stars.

Look not to the stars
For signs of the times.
Jesus said they are not ours
Therein to confide.
Astrology is blind.
One can only live in heaven…

By living in prayer on his knees.
No castle made of steel
Can set the spirit free.
The signs of the times
Say what will be!

HE WON'T SUFFER YOU

I was lost in temptations of the world
I had lost all control
And bound for hell, I cannot lie
Till Jesus saved my soul.

But with temptation I will make a way of
Escape. That you will be able to bear it.
So down on my knees, begging Him please…
Till now I am able to share it.

Jesus is faithful and Just.
He will not suffer you beyond what you
Are able. Just get on your knees
Down on your knees before the Lord.

I was corrupted, carried by the desires of my heart
Living by this world of sin,
Bound for hell, till Christ saved my soul
When I let His Holy Spirit in.

He will make a way of escape
That you will be able to bear it
He won't suffer you
So, you can be around to share it…

Eternal life.

ONE GREAT SONG

I can't see it any more
Must have lost my mind
Just sink me below earths floor.
So tired of doing time.

The radio is grand
My mate so many nights
But that one, one great song
Cuts me like a knife.

I can get along just great
Till I hear such feeling in a song
My spirit long then, not to wait
Just go ahead and get it on.

Get it over with
I can't take it any more
My heart betrayed its' gift
Now it's so sad and sore.

But onward the band must play.
Behind laws my talent mimes.
But I got to go on like this.
So tired of doing time!

ONCE UPON A WINDY WAYSIDE

Who can look at river water?
And say if it's warm or cold,
Unless it's frozen or boiling
You must touch it to know.

Once upon a windy wayside
I met a mother of none
She appeared to be angry
So, I moved to let her go.

Along came a jolly fellow:
I still know that he knew
Who can look at the water?
And say that it's warm or cold?

With a gentle word, he touched her
And boys, she broke as glass, into a sweat
As she gave *me* the good-bye wav
 I realized I wasn't her crave.

You cannot look at the water
And say if it's warm or cold.
Unless it's frozen or boiling
You must touch it to know.

DEATH OF A PRIME MINISTER

When out of good comes evil
What song is left to sing:
When in the land of choice, a believer
Assassinates a king?

Ideate conspirators
Politics on street "Of Red".
They say the reverend soldiers
Are those who are dead?

Shalt thou not kill,
When it's written for the lot?
Do not believe that peace is dead
All must be fulfilled to the jot.

Peace has always been gunned down,
Since Abel's blood cried forth from the ground.
But when out of good, comes evil sting
What song is left to sing?

I'm just a foolish imprisoned poet
Not President, Prime Minister nor King.
Which of these can define peace?
In only their deaths, by its desirous increase!

POETS LIFE

Carpenters ache form blisters burns.
Congressional representatives handle, "The Big Wheel" that turns.
A preacher's hand knows your spirit calls.
Presidents fear the impact, when their country falls.

A poet rubs all that flows
His heartbeat is the entire world
The forest green and desert snow
Whose heart is gnawed by man and Lord.

Gourmet chefs relish lively spice.
Asian cultures, tuna and rice,
Rich man savior's delicacies.
If a poor man eats, his heart agrees.

Yet the poet's gusto is all of these:
Sipping to know the morsel of life
Asian steak, to honey of bees.
The poet's flavor is the world of device.

To mortician's noses, all things are death.
To a doctor's sinuses all is newborn breath.
Stain on banker's suit, all is haste.
To plumbers, all of life is waste.

Yet the poet's scent is the world renown.
Perfumed foul or rotten sweat.
The sense of rain or summer's heat.
To know the world from one small town.

An artist peers through artists' eyes
A musician's view finds where music lies.
Psychologist leer toward hypnotized.
Philosophers apprise to justify.

The poet's mind is all of these.
Gazing through his neighbor's eyes,
The big blue sky and deep blue seas.
Poet's heed universal guise.

Prejudice ears know racial slurs.
Love comes not by, such sounds blurred.
Angers ears await the fight.
As wisdom trains to reach new heights.

While to poet's ears', nature sings.
Her lyrics cover all these things.
For the poet is but natures tool.
When she sings, he is her biggest fool.

A CENTURY OF STYLE
(EULOGY TO GEORGE BURNS)

"Now that it's all over for you
We're mourning the loss".
All pictures have ceased with George,
You were a century of style.
All the world will be missing your face.
The big show has ended.
The stage is now silent with tear.
Your reflection.
You will always be here,
In the hearts of the worldwide.
Up, on the screen you stood smiling.
On the ground I smiled too.
Compiling your jokes and gesture for a laugh.
And I learned to smile this I liked.
Now I also make people smile.
Because you were a Century of Style.

WHAT HAVE I?

What have I to hold?
Close to my heart so dear
Keeping me from cold
Are memories so near

Memories of you, babe
I've treasured for so long
Live now a-new
I feel thee grow me strong

Held here in my heart
Proliferations cell
Reproducing art
My art is all for you

What have I to hold?
I've kept you in my heart
Don't see me as bold
I want you to be my wife

Here, a heart of waif;
By lure and love not bruised;
For I have held it safe
And offer it to you…

THE MAKE PUZZLE THEORY

They sometimes flashed by with a daunting speed:
Those hard to see, behind trees and corners:
Others that came on strong from a distance,
Making their statement from afar
"Look, here am I, see what I can say"

Overhead, to the left or on the right
Tall and wide or short and skinny, etc. etc.
Each with a statement and one choice.
Do this, do that, each would persuade.
Two choices, look or turn your eyes away.

I tried to notice in everyone.
Just to try to recognize one central thought
Like food, gas, rest, or ice or market.
Malls were fun, with all sorts of toys and lots of reading
But seldom encountered with these eyes, their inside

Obsessed, Infatuated, I was at awe
(So many things there which I couldn't see)
Obsessed so that I'd study oncoming, and back even
Then make puzzles of what the other side might hold.
Breakneck shapes at seventy miles per hour.

With some of nights light to read at night
But that was guidance time working out directions.
We sometimes missed a road or two,
Because I was by conserving the lit-up show
I was only six, learning to read on the highways!

3-20-1996

THE CITY DUMP

Red-brown breathing pie crust
Scarred by a D-9 tracked CAT.
Papier Mache fence line, like Japanese
Bunker Hill solders
Unbending to weight.
Bottles now, think bottles!
Ten cents for each
Coke or Pepsi
Bronze Bouillon
Used for the junk food.
Once the trash was dumped
Wanting to bring home everything that did
Look interesting:
A one-armed solder,
A three-wheeled wagon,
Some hungry dog, dagger, or poorer than poor
Digging for food.

An Everest of trash,
A hand full of treasure
A pit of production, economy, past and future
Accomplishment.

One layer of life
One layer of earth
An essential of the world,
Essential of man.

The sad looking face
Will always
In my young heart have
Its place!

JARGON

Rocking my brain
Going insane
Numbing the pain
With a refrain.

Here I go again
Losing to win
Chose to sin
Best not pretend.

Musical hands
Un-useful sands
In the wind
Arrow with bend.

Taxing my mind
Jargon to find
Insight combined
Helps me unwind.

SEE AMERICA (NEO ART)

Come and see America world
Best come prepared to run
Don't walk the streets late at night
Lest you be victim to a hating gun

Another tourist gunned down yesterday
Hate must need another hit of crack
The child whose wish was, to visit the free world
It took a lifetime for a bullet in the back

Come to take foot in this fair land?
Just don't ever visit around March
First take a good look around
What you'll find isn't art

What you will find are filthy streets
People tend to take all they need
Some addict in a greed
Looking for a tourist to gun down

Come look at America fan
Better have a weapon at hand
What you will find is neo art
For the love of gold not of the heart.

SLEEP SONG

My neighbor used to tell me
"Man, you sleep too much".
Get back to reality
And those dreams will hush

But I found another diamond
Dawn below the coal
Each time I reach to grab it
Something awakes to break my hold

I must always visit dream world
Where my jewels are hiding
So, when you hear me, sleep talking
Just pass on by my bed

There's lots of restful sleeping
In a lot of king-sized beds
But I have trouble keeping
My feet from hanging off the edge

I hear that bed a calling
Like an old and long-lost friend
To tell me tales of genius
That are so difficult to comprehend

When forever I am able
Just to sleep and dream
Let me alone
It's the only time I'm clean.

GYPSIES AND THIEVES

Modern day cowboys no longer hang 'round
Riding the planes, like ole Jesse James,
Society's gypsies and thieves with no town
Cowboys and outlaws ride free as the sound.

Converse with my horse for lonely ole nights
Bacon and coffee made for a good day
Forty miles per sun on a hand full of hay
From city to city, two irons in flight.

Modern day cowboy
Named by society, gypsies and thieves
Taking life by the reins all along
Cowboys and outlaws weren't always at wrong

Some thieves today are called hero
Just let them ride off into the wind.
They had to shoot Jesse, he had to go.
Butch and Sundance were also too slow.

They saddled the flame right from their hell
John Wesley Harden, he fit the bill
Still roaming the planes up to the date
Modern day cowboys are not all late

Some say they were overly bold.
Bring in the new so one more tale is told
Some of them boys were never gunned down
Bat and Doc need to return, to clean up the town.

BREATHING GOWN

I heard a rumble that would not stop
Crumbling for many hours
It's been thundering
Rolling up the clouds

The universe is shaken
Deep beneath its mounds
Everything's been quaking
Just can't forget that sound

It's been thundering
Then awaiting lightening
At any time to hit the ground
Of a universe that's dying

Everything shaken back to noun
Just as we first encountered
Before it mannered
That we were even found

It's been thundering
An oversized clapping
Before an audience
Of eminent bounds

Rolling up the door mat
Rolling up the clouds
It's been thundering
Something disturbed the powers

Picking up my properties
None left to write it down
Rolling up the universe
Rolling up lights gown

And the thunder roared
It's been thundering
Rolling up the town
Rolling up this breathing gown.

FLESH

If a god of flesh
Had roamed for four hundred years
Doing whatever gods do.

Upon encountering a female
Also, that of godly flesh
Who could consider, but that:

Would it matter? Of any difference
About her state, appearance
Or background?

To roam in deserts and be dry
For too many days
To happen across a drink

Would it matter, of what type or taste?
If it changed his state of mind
Or put him to sleep?

Would it make a difference?
To be cold or stale,
Would it matter to be, ail?

Would life today make him frown?
Or would it make him grin
Would he care to come again?

AUTHENTICITY

Authenticity
You needn't search for
We're born with it.
Your grand masters mind,
My simplicity
Doesn't make the grade.
For once I knew a man
Whom was considered dumb!
That he was only unique
Made no means: the chores
All over his face:
But unlike my friend
WE can see our gift,
For just what it is.
So, we polish and shine
And build on it
Houses of straw.
I don't believe in fate,
Nor destiny
But someone must be
Authenticity.

PAIN IN HAPPINESS

Do not touch the rose bush!
Don't stand out in the rain!
Yeah! But what if
Even with the gift
I don't know how to live without pain?

For some it's kind of useful
Not necessarily a charm
But was it not for this?
I could know no happiness
For they do walk arm in arm.

One time I tried to forget
About this knowing ache inside
Then all my joy disappeared
Which I so greatly feared
By neither of the two can we abide.

Sometimes it hurts to be happy
At another, I may laugh when I'm sad
Yet when I'm depressed, I claim "Ah yes!"
For the joy of what another page obtains
I just don't know how to live without pain!

SONNETS AND SIMI SONNETS (APPROXIMATELY 1993-1999)

For what? Are the days in joyous youth!
When none does focus eyes; seeing we do not see,
Therein our nature's beauty, or lessons gave.
The mind so wonders to-and-fro, uncouth.
Ardor-less School becomes a game to be
Next to cradled anilities. We crave
Just solace, given by the pal of a toy.
This past, well obligated to fade,
Lights on as the storm, as the ground be fed.
This fairest haven, a shame we must envoi,
Step the step from maternal shade
With our focus to employ ahead
Stepping into the turning lath of earth.
Which jambs all that thirst to stir its mirth.

Here stands the day upon my breast,
I have addressed the stars
Concerning your pure faithfulness
In the times which once was ours.
Those pilgrimages to party stone
The sky would flourish into a whale,
Castles, crawling tanks;
Sometimes we were just alone.
Often now I think:
Stillness fills around about me the air
And I awake…
Here I lay, Simmer Lake
DE-vanced into a shell
But all is good and tame: justice is well!

Stern mountains are the years
When age upon your heart is piled
And death trickles nearer, your place to hold:
Where youth is young no more, many fear
All the horrors told him can drive the rack wild
When you have nothing for to grasp a hold;

A walking mount of cruel deeds;
Where death comes marching nigh,
His senses spry, alert the essence of his being
And he fears (the child seeing a devil in the weeds)
Fear grips a lonely heart, would make a stone to cry
But before he comes for your deeds
Be back to fulfill your dreams, yourself to redeem.

One single life holds no immortal range
Things longed the heart full, therein to succeed
No present stranger to old coins of change
Will strives within until the end proceeds
Reach, take hold the star dangled off some visage
Great measure what trump must achieve
Well fancies man some elasticity to manage
However far passage; whatever you believe
Old darkness must settle eagles claim.
Green lawn of pure haven, sure all he reached
Take heed then that after his wings were lame
Skies length, it's realized there is no breach
When he looks to grounds where serpents lie
It's one single life, but still he flies.

Enchanting jaunts to party stone
Lost in plains of sophistry alone
The sky would flourish formative whales,
A crawling tank, or ship assail
Your castle of cloud does now haunt the so
That none can see mixtures of foam above

And not think of magical smiles
Heavy is this ingle heart within
History shaded in similes
The will is always a fawning dove
Will always be my castle above
Always will I walk that extra mile
Transit jolt of age does await the haul
My jaunt back to castles tall.

Mamma
What have I done?
Sat my house upon the desert
Blinded not by the Son
Set up my walls of Lego

So easily they snapped together
Though when the hard winds came
Howling my name
They bended my frame forever

Living in that plastic world
Quick assembly was such fun
Foundation was of caustic though
And kept me on the run

Living in a land of Lego
I plasticized my heart
The house, it had clean windows
Yet as it went un-kept, few saw.

It doesn't even need to be tomorrow
Makes no difference rain or shine
Talking through these walls to myself again
Looking only to waist less time.
It could at least be somewhat better:
A simple hello, good-bye.

Then again, I'm sure
There's much better entertainment
Then watching a man slowly die.

Days here forever have no meaning
If only I could know you tried
To write would make me better
Should it even be stamped with lies?
It doesn't even need to be tomorrow
I would cherish even letters of hate
Just as long as you show that you think of me
It doesn't even need to show love, only write me!

When there is no heart to speak to
Whom you may trust
When the skies may burst
And bleed war from your eyes
Your night tears fleet ships
Across your desert heart skies
Extinguishing volcanoes
That babies float safely in wicker baskets.

When you notice all and see nothing
You see all and notice everything
Trees stand tall in a forest that exist not
Hear the forest call, which isn't there.
When skies are unclouded and you see no blue
But blue is all you see
And blue is all you feel.

Everything has a price
What wages we do pay
If money cannot buy it, man play hell
But all the same, just as well
You will pay what you owe, some way.

Everything has a price
Throwing life on the toss of a dice
Though you're wearing boxcars mister
It's a little late to weigh!

Everything is a pact
The roots of your sickness aren't just money
You might as well face the fact
Roots run down the earth's core
Imagine that
All the bread this cruel world holds
Will amount to a pile of crop
Everything has a pact
When there are only upright walking animals
In a slow-moving trap.

Quit not the abacus Spryling
Their abattoir disconnects the soul
Bare flesh melts against a burning sun
To be an Aztec with Balaam;
Your howl could echo true
But the abbot to wagon idols idles
Abdicate your visions to rule.

Passed forth form the abdomen of earth
The theory of attention of all universe
Kidnapped by amoral vultures -
Paper gold, action love, reef roses
All melt any flesh bare
Ablution from Balaam
Empty wagons make much noise.

Springs of youth will nourish old trees
Where winds of reason walk in silence
Knowing no need of noise to rule
The self is health enough

To gather igniting intuit reason
That lights the corner of the vultures
For them to commit their treason.

You care to TALK TURKEY,
Chew the fat of BEEF JERKY!
And say that God SPARED YOUR LIFE!
You don't really WANT TO HEAR.
Well let me butterfly your ear,
You don't WANT to hear!
You have a family, have a wife;
And your piteous aggression condemns another
Unable to accept him as your brother:
So, you waddle on your merciless ways, IN STRIFE.
You DON'T EVEN UNDERSTAND GOD
Much less PRECIOUS LIFE.
You mutter desire to talk turkey.
You don't want to hear my side!
THE TRUTH!
YOU DO NOT LIKE TO BARE
Because of frivolous, FEVERISH FEAR;
Or your reason of, WHATEVER?
To make you condemn one who does try
While you lay back, sandy heart so dry
And gratify yourself to CONDEMN.
You don't want to hear!
CONTENTLY THINKING GOD
For the twenty-five years!
Placed upon my life.
The words you spit at me
In their decaying spirit of
Acid Tongue.
Only make me stronger!
NO! You don't want to hear
Why I was mad!
This old stone has been baked in a furnace

Let me tell you that is real
Burned and covered in icing
Like a commercial disguise
Filled with lies
Called a deal!

Time, time after time!
Have I crossed these States!
Too many times, passed through the gates.
Night after night laid awake and cried
Eaten crow- Swallowed pride
In great hope to soon be whole again.
Years, year upon year, slowly pass me by
Showing on my face
My aging inside.
Tears have rivered so long
Their lakes are desert dry.
I've cried my foolish heart out
Over lessons and lies.

March! Still, I march
Onward to the prize
If they're seen only with my eye.
For the love of God, I march
For a mansion in the sky.
I have weathered a thousand storms
Through barred windows at night
Seasons go and come
Eclipse of the sun
All slowly pass me by.
Though when it is all over
I still, and will have Eternal Life…

To bed, to again hoist your dreams
With no recognizable trace
Soon will be a revised text.

A new scene, modem and motive.
The tongues that would address your face
Will address another.
You walked your valley, did your passage
Through the ill minds' virtues of sophistry.
Tongues with trails of lag
Infecting where their whim may choose
To lead in reply of automation
Your clock now tolls new hands
And one day will toll patronage
Annulling there your history.

Two trees stand luminary
Together, apart, in a soil by roots
Digging deep below the surface
Of the dirt that covers your connections
Sometimes getting at the darkest truths
Just to see the light.
Do we play to win, or pass the test?
Knowing the value of the loss
On the constant thresh hold of zest
An innocent threat of relapse
When allowed the mind to rest
Bleed a root pickled heart, when allowed
Blotched by elfin, the mind to rest
Beating nubile drums, repose no grasp
Deem it best, the past not to wizen

Who Would offer understanding help
In assisting lions to learn to yelp?
So, herein assert some decree.
To share, ridding beaches of their kelp.
Pondering its profound mystery.
Lighting blot shade
Of some haunting histories.
From first essential afraid

To a final felling-less fear.
I plan to utilize my way
To help accurately steer
Mystery to pylon By the apples of knowledge compiled
Gratefully assent to cross the miles.

Before me: through the eyes you see, my peers
Before you I dedicate my years
To the Everest interest wherein harmonized
Those whose respects rightly revere
And care rightly tries
To make the heart pure and true
Before grown old or younger die.
So herein my mightier than sword drew
Flays the rent of illusions vale
Where are pent visions through?
Perceivers must not fail
To help non-scientism scienter afar
Beyond the mightiest mask
For every reverie had this task.

Consider fleas in a brown glass jar
Before glass is removed, they give up on jumping to par.
No insight that light mans it is clear
To step out for going far.
So careful to speak just the right.
Searching empirical ink, afore laid down
Assuredly precise, pent attributes
Help us all stay off the ground.
By readers eyes light computes.
For mine it is a telling story,
No fables, merely perceptions pioneer
In steering the pen, so many years.

Not parlayed so heavily hoary
About pain, agony, Spirit and worry

During all of which
I give my best
To send our harmonization to the crematory
Peers agonize by its weight a-chest
, Fear not to share the lights oil in my cup
To be sincere and attest Assiduous hiccup.
Communication; is the key to peace,
Not war, hate, or "I'll beat you up".
But the inner calming of the beast
By embalming dark benign.
"If I am wise", I agree with Socrates' ambivalence
"It's because I am more aware of my ignorance."

12-20-1995

Printed in the USA
CPSIA information can be obtained
at www.ICGtesting.com
CBHW020103190824
13304CB00044B/698